# What People Say
## Praise for Ed Wood the entrepreneur

'Ed's wise counsel and considered opinion have been immensely helpful in getting our business on the right track over the last two years.'

'Ed has been an indispensable strategic thinker and business partner in the last few years. His diligence, attention to detail, and clarity of thought have brought great dividends. His incisive approach to inevitable challenges, creating instant solutions, has been a revelation.'

'Ed has been invaluable to us. To have someone who is not only entrepreneurial, but also a Chartered Accountant by trade, is the ultimate combination for a business. He provides utterly sound advice, reassurance, has a wealth of solid experience and can give an alternative opinion when the bigger picture is needed. Every business should have an Ed if they want to thrive!

'Ed is a true gentleman, with the outstanding ability to engineer a difficult situation into one of clarity. He is cool, calm and collected, with the ability to help in all aspects of business, from drawing up a business plan to helping to resolve petty issues.'

'Part granular analysis, part strategic thinking, part informed sounding board, part friendly encouragement and support, Ed is at his best when flushing out all the interconnected factors that come together to create the particular business crisis at hand.'

'Ed is an intuitive, quick problem-solver, asking pertinent questions and coming up with realistic solutions. He brings with him a huge amount of experience. We've delved into and analysed our finances and he has helped us develop an immediate and long-term plan. We're already seeing great results in organisation and profitability.'

# LIFT OFF!

Ed Wood

# LIFT OFF!

## GETTING BUSINESS OFF THE GROUND

Ed Wood

RUNWAY
PUBLISHING

**RUNWAY**
PUBLISHING

Published by Runway Publishing

www.runwaypublishing.co.uk

First edition, May 2021

©Runway Publishing, 2021

ISBN: 978-1-8384901-0-2

This book is dedicated
my father, Richard, whose
example of strength, coupled
with everlasting patience,
I continue to try to follow.

# Contents

# ACKNOWLEDGEMENTS

## Bringing It All Together

There's a paradox at the heart of life as an entrepreneur. There's more aloneness in this vocation—and it is a vocation, I believe—than in a career spent in large companies. You often feel like the only person on the bridge. And yet, to be an entrepreneur, a successful one—by which I mean one who experiences failure and error and learns to adapt along the way—you are undoubtedly the collection of all that you are. You bring every experience, every person, every moment of learning, into everything you do. And in my case, after nearly 50 years in business, that means a lot of people who have helped me along the way.

I wish to start this book with these acknowledgements to encourage you, as you build your own business, to instil the same ethos in your own growth. Just as we keep records of financial profits, so, too, must the human profits be logged. My acknowledgement list here contains both positive and negative moments; but as an entrepreneur, they are of equal benefit. Without these attempts to help me—or trip me up—I would not know enough to have written this book.

To begin at the beginning: my father. As a soldier in his twenties, a bomb landed on his legs, but luckily did not go off. It did, however, remove both of his legs above the knee. Showing amazing strength, he went on to make a great success of his life and to teach me the value of persistence, as well as his signature quiet patience. To reflect on someone, who was a very good athlete, being crippled at such a young age, and then going on to be a successful politician, with the enormous strains imposed by that role, made a massive impact on me. If my father could turn his life around so dramatically, then so could I, without any such disability, when I encountered failures and near disasters.

I have always responded defiantly to the criticism of others, which can so often be the grit for the pearl... and so it was, too, in my training to be a Chartered Accountant (a big mountain if you failed your Maths O-Level twice, as I did) when my tutor, Alastair Kennedy, told me I would never qualify. So, of course, I dug deep and did just that—with thanks to the kindness of another tutor, John Moffat, who has permanent membership of my hall of fame for helping me crack the subject that had me most stumped.

And, so, into professional life. Thanks to most bankers, I learnt who not to trust. Thanks to hoodwinkers in my time in property, I learnt how to out-think obstacles and competitors. A foray into politics taught me how to argue—and also negotiate. As a Central London magistrate, I learnt to listen and make wise judgements. Just a handful of the myriad encounters and connections with people who have added a little something to enable me to crack the code of entrepreneurship—and life itself—a bit more effectively.

To round all things entrepreneurial off here, I want to thank Miranda Khadr, highly valued client of Runway Advisors, fellow Runway Advisor, and reviewer of *Lift Off!*. I asked Miranda if she would review this book, which she very kindly agreed to do, having read it painstakingly from cover to cover and suggested some very insightful changes which have made *Lift Off!* a lot better.

The reason I asked her to do this is because she fits the bill as a model for what this book is about. She is an entrepreneur, through and through, with the courage, and integrity, to climb the mountains she sets out to conquer, and the leadership qualities to nurture her fellow climbers with her along the journey. Miranda, already a very successful loan broker, is the founder of Pitch 4 Finance—the very first interactive online platform of its kind—bringing lenders, intermediaries and borrowers together, in one place, to enable lenders to showcase their products and do deals with customers online.

For a time, I flew helicopters. What a huge amount of learning I found there: how to develop a very cool nerve under pressure—and survive on several occasions when I should not have done.

In my reading life, I owe much to the writings of

Michael Gerber, Robert Townsend, Chris Voss, Peter Thiel, Robert Cialdini, Stephen Pressfield, Dr Ranjan Chatterjee, B J Fogg, George Clason, Harv Eker, Brian Tracey, Steven Covey and James Altucher, among many others, whose books have guided me greatly in my lifetime's study of entrepreneurship—which is very much ongoing!

And in my writing life, my thanks to my editor, Holly Dawson, whose patience, humour and sheer editorial skill have also earned her a place in my personal hall of fame as my indisputable muse.

In my personal life, more learning, more discovery. A divorce that both toughened me up and softened me and made me more forgiving. My darling wife Katha has imbued my life with more wisdom and wellbeing than she can know; while my four wonderful daughters, Leo, Georgie, Ella and Jemima, and my granddaughters, Evie and Frankie, have taught me not only what is important, but—even more importantly—how to laugh at myself (or they would do it for me).

Before you get stuck into the pages of this book, I recommend you take a moment to reflect on who and what has made you who you are. And be sure to include your low points. My many failures, some of which I share candidly with you in this book, have taught me far more than the successes I have been lucky enough to enjoy. Most importantly, among all of these, is to never, ever, give up.

I hope that you may read on with openness. The main trait of a good entrepreneur is their ability to reflect and to learn. So, I hope, above all, that you may find something in this book to help you along the path that lies ahead of you.

‘ The most difficult thing
is the decision to act.
The rest is mere tenacity ’

Amelia Earhart

The first female aviator to fly solo across the Atlantic Ocean.
Born: 24 July 1897, Atchison, Kansas, United States.
Disappeared: July 2, 1937 (aged 39); Pacific Ocean, en
route to Howland Island from Lae, Papua New Guinea

# FOREWORD

Most of the time when I was involved in writing this book, the world was battened down, combating coronavirus.

An event, like the arrival of Covid-19, comes once in a lifetime, and there will be plenty of lifetimes which have not seen such a thing.

Some businesses, if they were very lucky, have been dealt opportunities by Covid, which have been very helpful to them. The vast majority have not.

During this time, so much has depended, and will continue to depend on business owners being seriously inventive. And praying for a huge helping of luck on top. There are many wonderful examples emerging, that show how agile, small and local businesses are in fact well-placed to help at this time: the brewery that switches to making hand sanitiser, the clothing brand that gets its team making NHS scrubs, the food companies prepping nourishing food to deliver to hospital staff for free. Some online brands have prioritised community-building over selling, keeping their followers sane at a disconcerting time. All these strategies boost positive brand reputation—and will convert into new and loyal customers when spending returns.

As we putter our way, with throttled back engines, through these uncharted waters, here are some thoughts to make challenges feel less insurmountable:

1. Accept that you have no control of the situation. Let go and try and find peace.
2. Forget trying to plan too much. Things change so fast. Be ready to change with them.
3. Try not to be angry with the situation, with the government, with people. Accept the situation. Those things, which you cannot change, will get easier.
4. Avoid the media. It will drive you crazy—if it has not done so already!
5. Find that sense of community. This is a time when we can choose who to spend our energy on—and with—who we want to call, message, connect with. Watch the quality of our relationships improve.
6. Appreciate this forced downtime. When do you ever have time like this? When will you have it again? Will you miss it when we go back to the fast-pace of the real world? Time goes so fast. And it doesn't return.
7. Savour and enjoy the little things of every day. Live in the present. Notice and be grateful for them.

8.   Get into good physical shape. Here is your chance. Eat good food. Drink lots of water. Take gentle daily exercise. Get at least eight hours sleep each night. Avoid stress.

9.   This is a chance to get on better every day with other members of our families, who may, like mine, be sharing our isolation.

10.  See this as a chance to reach others. Helping others makes us feel better. Every time. And...

11.  Perhaps ponder how things might be done differently in the new world into which we will, sooner or later, emerge.

On a business level, it is vital we think ahead to what the new normal might be. How can you make sure your company can be prepared and ahead of the curve?

I believe we will continue to do a lot more remote working. We have discovered Zoom and how useful it is for conferences and calls. People are getting comfortable with it, even if they are now ready to spend more time 'at the water fountain'. Habits stick. We may find that we become more efficient without travelling to endless meetings. We save money. We get things done. More Zoom, less zooming around.

We have seen a surge in remote learning. Traditionally the poor cousin to face-to-face training, it has just received a huge shot in the arm. This can only be a great thing.

Disruptive tech is booming. The pandemic accelerates advances in robotics, drones and machines. How will they change the shape of your industry? Are you well-placed to embrace them, and change as your sector changes? Is there an opportunity here for you to innovate and create new ways to do what you do well?

Alongside this increased reliance on good tech comes a greater awareness of community and people. Covid is teaching us what really matters and how to nurture our relationships and keep people close. This should include our customers and clients. The connected economy will become more important than ever. When your audience start returning to you, they may require more reassurance, more trust, more support. Be grateful for those who return. You'll need them more than ever before.

We do business better when we are living and working in a connected way. This isn't pseudo-hippy speak— look after yourself, and your work capacity will improve. Look after your commercial community and it will convert to loyal customers and brand ambassadors.

And most importantly for the entrepreneur—this is a time to learn, learn, learn. If it hits you hard, as it has many of us, how can you climb your way back up? How can this time of difficulty become an opportunity? What do you want your world to look like on the other side?

# PREFACE

## WALKING AWAY FROM THE SCENE OF THE CRASH

**Monday 12 November, 2012, Worcester County Court**

I am standing, with my wife Katha, outside Worcester County Court. Visibility is poor, and the rain drizzling down, as we park our car and make our way up the steps to the court, shivering under my umbrella.

This is a day I have dreaded, just as I once dreaded divorce, until it happened. And dreaded going to prison or getting cancer—neither of which have transpired, and touch wood, never will.

Our purpose this morning is to declare personal bankruptcy. It is rare to be called in front of the judge before he makes such an order, but we are duly called.

Judge Kitto is a lovely man with a kind look about him. He speaks to Katha and me, in his rooms, in a quiet voice, asking us if there is really no other way out of our situation. I tell him what has led us to this point. He says: 'I see, you have simply run out of cash. Very well, then, I will make these orders, and I wish you much better times ahead. I feel sure you will find them.'

Our business there takes less than an hour. We walk back to the car, feeling utterly numb.

Five years of struggling with a property investment portfolio, hard hit by the credit crunch, has ended in defeat. I am sixty-one. My confidence is knocked sideways. I can see no future ahead.

Our bank accounts are frozen. I have to surrender my hard-earned qualification as a Chartered Accountant. Both Katha and I have to submit to intense interrogation by the Official Receiver. Bankruptcy takes away our freedom of movement—everything we do takes a lot longer and is a lot harder.

Just when we need a break, we don't get one. We had spent two long years, before this moment, wrestling every which way to avoid it happening. When bankruptcy was first suggested, I had flinched from it with a sick feeling in my stomach. We had tried being resourceful. We had tried sorting things out, and staying positive. But we had been in too deep. Our portfolio of 150 buy-to-let properties, acquired during the good years leading up to the crash, had quickly haemorrhaged money in the bad years that followed. We thought our appearance in court was the end of that journey. But it turns out to be the beginning of a new one.

# The Long Climb

Later that day, I break a pair of hearing-aids, and claim for them from the NFU. They repudiate my claim because I am 'a bankrupt' (I hate the *a* that turns our circumstances from something that happened, into something we *are*). 'I didn't know I had to declare that,' I say. 'Oh, yes,'... they tell me. 'You do.' And so, they don't pay out. We have joined the ranks of the statistically unreliable—a throwback from the days of the old debtors' prison.

Elsewhere—compassion. I ring my hearing-aid supplier and explain the situation. For a new pair, without insurance, I will have to fork out five thousand quid. I don't have that. Not even a spare five hundred. I'll never forget what they said: 'Your credit is good here, Ed, pay us when you can.'

The guys who financed my Mercedes are the same. 'Keep the car, Mr Wood, you were right up there. It doesn't take a rocket scientist to see you'll get back there.'

I am eternally grateful to both of them. They give me a trace of hope.

Moments of kindness like this lift us during the long climb ahead. We are quite unprepared for the early stages of that climb and we find little solace in experts. Insolvency lawyers know quite a bit about bankruptcy, but, in the main, not having themselves been declared bankrupt, they have little to share on the subject of the experience itself any more than an undertaker can tell you what it feels like to be dead. With bankruptcy, however, *can* come resurrection. That, you have to learn for yourself. And we start to do so, slowly but surely.

Our lifestyle changes drastically. Katha and the girls are amazing. We watch a lot of movies at home. Our beloved horses and terriers keep us sane when we cannot afford to entertain or to go on holiday. We are forced to take our three daughters out of the private school system and put them into state education—luckily, the academy close to us serves them well, in many ways, and gives them the push to get some very good qualifications, as well as teaching them a lot about life and driving them into a tremendous work ethic.

The pain takes a lot of getting over. It is a huge personal and professional transition for us all. And devastating for our family. We have no idea what the future will hold. During these dark days, our wider family help us beyond the call of duty. I shall remain truly grateful for their immense kindnesses and extraordinary levels of understanding and support, without which we might not have made it through.

Apart from family, we tell very few people; only those we really trust, and some who need to know. Both, strictly confidentially. Bankruptcy still carries a stigma in the UK, rather like divorce once did. Not quite the shame of the debtor's prison, but a slimmed-down version of that. As a result, the B-word is not one which you share with just anybody. Having to keep this secret, while trying to keep up standards, keep our heads above water, keep our spirits up, brings an enormous added strain and more than a touch of loneliness and isolation. I am immensely burdened with guilt for taking Katha and the girls through this hell.

On 11<sup>th</sup> November, 2013, exactly one year after that dark rainy day in Worcester, we are discharged from bankruptcy. Less than six months after that, I am told I am being readmitted to the Institute of Chartered Accountants—a process that normally takes closer to three years. Bankruptcy was a cloud which I thought had no silver lining. I was wrong. Sometimes, bad luck is the best luck you will ever have. And, so it has turned out for me.

## Reframing Bankruptcy and Embracing Failure

Nearly eight years have now passed since we sat in Worcester Court. Looking back from this distance, in the rear-view mirror, I can clearly see how the experience brought with it great learning and growth. The lessons we learned, in both our business and personal lives, have been beyond price.

In America, bankruptcy is a rite of passage—just as it should be here. The Brits don't celebrate failure. They should. Failure tests us, strengthens us, teaches us real lessons worth learning. Lessons you don't learn in school.

It has taught me, above all, to take complete responsibility for my own actions. In my personal life, it has taught me to value and treasure relationships so much more, and to truly appreciate the little things in life. To fully live in the present.

In business, I have taken this as the opportunity to help other small-to-medium-sized businesses to survive, to become more profitable, and to have more fun on their journeys, by sharing with them the business lessons I have learned over almost 50 years.

We are now firmly back on terra firma, and all the more fleet of foot for what has happened. My advisory business has grown exponentially. My colleagues and I, at Runway Advisors (the collective I formed to help small companies grow) have many happy clients. I am having more fun in my work life than I can ever remember.

## Up, Up and Away

I found out myself—the hard way—that business can be lonely when you're the lead entrepreneur on the bridge. Especially when others are relying on you, and you don't have a foil, who is your equal, to kick things around with. In the years since that climb back from bankruptcy, I've grown to be pretty resourceful, solution-orientated, efficient and intuitive, with a good nose for picking winning strategies over losing ones (and there are, sadly, plenty of losing ones). Things often appear simple. And they can be. But I find that what I've learned over the years comes in very handy when they're not.

My experience comes from helping a range of businesses—to list but a few: nightclubs, property companies, rag trade, furniture, music festivals, rural estates, hospitality, renewable energy, technology, chiropractic, investment management, head hunting, drug detection, dress design, art restoration, reclamation, racehorse training, accountancy, banks, political lobbying, travel agency, fruit and vegetables, tea merchants, seed merchants, schools, motor trade, aggregates, breweries and more.

Something else has always been important to me, however, alongside my life in business—helicopters. I racked up about 2,000 flying hours, an experience which would shape my business ethos in many unexpected ways. I found it offered an excellent analogy for my work with clients. Flying requires constant focus and attention. The right skills and training for the cockpit. A clear and realistic direction. Your route may be troubled by obstacles, crises, unpredictable events. You need to keep a constant eye on cash—the fuel of business. Flying requires intuitive problem-solving, 24/7 to keep you airborne and on track. But once you are up there, in the sky, there is no thrill like it.

If we apply this to developing a new business—and if we expand the aviation metaphor to planes as well—we get four fundamental components:

- THE AIRCRAFT. This is the idea, the product or service—the business itself.
- THE PILOT, CO-PILOT AND CREW. The team that will keep it airborne.
- THE WINGS. This is how we market our products and get them out there into the world.
- THE ENGINE. This is simple: it's cash. If it runs out, we tend to fall out of the sky...

So it seemed natural to me to call this book *Lift Off!*—a user's guide to getting your business off the runway and up into level, enjoyable, safe flight.

I wish someone had written a book like this for me earlier in my career. Maybe I'd have avoided a few of those potholes I have fallen into, and wrong turnings I have taken, on the road to where I am today. My greatest hope is that you may find at least one idea within its pages, which will help you to increase your profits and enjoy your business even more. Maybe just one idea which can turn into a nugget of gold for you.

Without having gone bust, *Lift Off!* would not have been written; nor would I have learned so many lessons that would make it worth the writing. Without writing this book, I wouldn't now be speaking with you.

A few years ago, I was talking to Ted Nicholas, one of the world's greatest direct mail copywriters. He said this to me: 'Ed, remember this. What comes from the heart, goes to the heart, so please only ever write from the heart. If you can get one great idea across in any book that you write, it will make all the difference.'

I hope you will feel that I have written from the heart, and that you have been able to find that one good idea somewhere in these pages.

# CHAPTER ONE

# CHOOSING THE PILOT FOR YOUR AIRCRAFT

The title of this chapter may seem ridiculous: 'Me, Ed! I'm the pilot! This is my business after all.' But it's not always that simple.

Consider this question: What is an entrepreneur?

Nobody seems to know. And that is no great surprise. Why?

Because there is nobody out there to teach them. *Oh, yes there is*, I hear you think—*there's my accountant.* Or you might brightly say that your friend, who has just got his MBA, can help you. Or maybe your lawyer. Or perhaps that business consultant who somebody recommended. Or even the bank manager.

A flash of hope. Only to be dashed when you discover that they don't really know either. Let's be unkind, but probably totally accurate—very few of the above know the first thing about entrepreneurship.

I'm a Chartered Accountant. In 1981, when I qualified, I knew sweet zero about being an entrepreneur, even after several years as an articled clerk, working on a huge variety of large and small company audits, for a firm that kept merging with bigger firms, thus ever widening the scope of clients I was exposed to.

I didn't have a clue about the need to have a big vision while implementing little things; about how to work hard—and learn to delegate and supervise; how to over-promise *and* over-deliver; how to find a market and sell into it; how, and why, to love a business; how to stop getting angry; how to say yes *and* no; how to conserve scarce resources; *and* how to have fun. Or even *why* I needed to know these things.

I've got news for you. The only people who truly know entrepreneurship are the people who have learned it the hard way. Through the seat of their pants at the school of hard knocks.

I learned nothing about entrepreneurship from being an accountant. The accountant is generally not a friend to small businesses, because small businesses are perceived to be risky—and poor payers. In other words, the kind of clients that accountants generally don't want to take on.

Even if they do take them on, they normally shy away from handling bookkeeping, which is essential to providing those businesses with up-to-date information as a basis for better decision-making. Imagine wanting to build a house and going to a builder only to be told: 'Of course, delighted to help, but you'll have to go to someone else for the foundations, because we just don't get involved with foundations'.

The MBA will generally spout theory, and probably clever theory, but it usually won't save you from the risks of entrepreneurship—which are essential to understand to ensure safe passage. The business consultant might make the right noises, might take you a little closer to the mark than the MBA, but a lot of his or her help may be sourced from business backgrounds other than those of the start-up. And finally, it is unusual to find a lawyer with a good enough grip on the numbers to help you there.

So, it's no wonder that so many businesses fail.

## The Warrior Mindset

In *Tales of Power*, Carlos Castaneda reports Don Juan's teaching that: 'The warrior takes everything as a challenge, while the ordinary man takes everything as a blessing or a curse'. That's a pretty accurate description of an entrepreneur's life. If they cannot emulate that warrior, then, pretty soon, they will give up trying to be an entrepreneur, and go back to being employed.

And what a warrior the entrepreneur needs to be. Statistics differ about survival rates, and the timescales of survival in start-ups, but there seems to be general agreement that about 40% fail in the first year. If they survive one year, it appears that another 40% will fold within five years. After that, among the ones still left, a further 80% will fail in the next five-year period.

Let's put some figures on that. We'll assume that 100 businesses start on day one. A year later, there are 60 left. Four years later there are 36 left. And in the next five years, 80% of those survivors will have gone. So, by the end of year ten, just seven of the hundred, who started ten years earlier, will still be around.

And what sort of survival will that be?

Certainly, those making it through will acquire many battle scars along the way—and probably suffer other casualties in terms of energy, stress, quality of life, not to mention hard-earned cash.

Is there a better way? The answer is a resounding yes, and it was with the goal of helping to increase survival rates that this book was written—to help those starting up in business to have a better chance of survival than the average; to make money; and to have fun doing it.

By the way, in my view, anyone can learn to be an entrepreneur. You may say that you can't. If you say it loud enough, you'll believe it and therefore be right. As Henry Ford said, 'Whether you think you can, or you think you can't, you're right'. But, as with everything, you have to *learn* how to become an entrepreneur. How to become the pilot of your own aircraft—your business.

# Getting Off to a Flying Start

Having fallen into more pooh traps than I can count in my business career, and laboriously climbed out of them, I came across a wonderful book called *The E-Myth* by Michael Gerber, one of the world's leading authorities on helping small businesses to improve their chance of survival. Gerber comes up with four key messages in the book:

1. In the main, those starting businesses are labouring under an entrepreneurial myth;
2. It is possible to set up a well-oiled operation that can be largely self-running;
3. There are systems that can be put in place to run that business: and
4. There are business development processes to make two and three above happen...

In other words, there is a solution. A solution that enables truly outstanding results.

Before we start looking at how most businesses start, it's important to get something clear: I am NOT talking about well-funded start-ups. For instance, the kind where seasoned businessmen or women take a whole department from another business, with a tried and tested team in place, add a pre-arranged line of funding and... bingo. No—they do not need this book. I am talking, instead, of situations where a person with an idea gives up their job, raises a little money from family and friends, and pushes out from the shore. Like Peter.

## Meet Peter...

Peter has been in his job for a while—in, let's say, a motor repair garage. He doesn't really like being told what to do by a boss, in a company where ethics aren't great, where promotion seems slow, and where pay is indifferent. He meets Simon in the pub after work. Simon started his own company four years ago and is earning twice as much as Peter. He can afford better holidays. A seed is sown in Peter's head.

Peter chews the fat for a bit. He talks to his wife. She's scared, but she can also see that Peter is struggling. Eventually, Peter persuades her that he wants to leave the garage and start up his own. A family grub stake is found, premises to rent near home, and Peter is in business.

And that's where the fun doesn't start, because Peter isn't an entrepreneur. He's a technician. He's fired the boss and hired himself. To get free—and to earn the extra money the boss was earning out of him. Or, so he thought.

As Michael Gerber would put it, Peter was yet another technician 'suffering from an entrepreneurial seizure'. A man who thought, like so many others, that if you know the 'tech', then you know all you need to know.

But you don't.

If you want to go into business, in order to ensure that you work ON the business, not IN the business, you should go into a business where you CAN'T do the tech, so you have to hire someone else to do it, leaving you free to focus on the most important thing that an entrepreneur has to focus on: building the business.

Like poor Peter, most discover very quickly that the freedom they so wanted has turned into slavery. Like Peter, it dawns on them that they now have to do absolutely everything:

- Design the business
- Find and manage suppliers
- Find and nurture clients
- Provide quotations
- Supervise the work
- Send out invoices (and chase them up)
- Pay bills, handle the bank, manage the money
- Look after the premises
- Hire staff, pay staff, look after staff, deal with problems with staff, fire staff

...and the list goes on. And on.

From a closer look, it becomes obvious, fairly quickly, that even if you had the time to manage all the above areas, you almost certainly would not have all the skills you would need to do so.

Like Peter, the exhilaration of being your own boss turns first to terror, then to exhaustion and, finally, to despair. Eventually, the technician in you realises that you have to be the manager, you have to put in the systems, you have to sweep up behind you. Like Peter, you started out the forward-thinking entrepreneur, went back to being the technician, and then realised you had to be the manager too—all at once. And, at that point, the trap sprang, and you could see no way out. Your dream had become a prison.

## The Impossibility of Being Three People

Peter, and countless others like him, suddenly realise that to run a business, you have to be three people:

- THE ENTREPRENEUR (who lives in the future)
- THE TECHNICIAN (who lives in the present) and
- THE MANAGER (who lives in the past)

In this tripartite struggle, it is almost impossible to succeed. Unless you quickly realise, having identified the Entrepreneur, the Technician and the Manager in you, that you must learn, and fast, how to perform all three roles at the same time.

The problem for us all is that we are almost certainly imbalanced as far as each of our individual abilities as Technician, Manager and Entrepreneur go.

- THE TECHNICIANS are doers not dreamers. They just do. They're happy working on one thing at once. They don't like bosses who push too hard. They live in the present. Everyone gets in their way. Especially Entrepreneurs. They are frustrated by interruptions. They find systems cold and inconvenient.

- THE MANAGERS know that, without them, the place would implode. They know that, without planning, without order, without predictability, the business would fall apart. They live in the past and crave order. They see work as a system of results.

- THE ENTREPRENEURS are different again. Very different. They are the leaders, the visionaries, the dreamers. The ones with the imagination and energy. The catalysts, who live in the future. The grand strategists. The creators of new things. They see probabilities out of possibilities. They want to control everything. And, in the process, create havoc for others to clear up.

# Evolving into an Entrepreneur

As I said before, anybody can be an entrepreneur. That's still correct. There are certain attitudes and attributes which successful entrepreneurs share. Right now, you may have some of them, all of them, or very few. You might be more Technician, more Manager, or a bit of all three. That doesn't matter. What matters is your willingness to learn. To grow into the Entrepreneur's shoes. To know what you are striving for and work on those qualities no matter what...

So how do we do that?

I. **Lead the Way**

The first and most important of these attributes is to be able to act like a leader. Leadership requires very different actions to those required from a Manager. The leader needs to be authentic, trustworthy, able to build strong relationships, exercise sound judgement, communicate well, take decisions without dithering, inspire others and, also, be humble and truly himself, or herself, at all times. Relax and breathe. Always be prepared for change. Remember that the pain of change always leads to a bigger and more abundant world for all. But it does not come without pain. Pain and change are fellow travellers on the journey of both entrepreneurship (and life) and are thus unavoidable. So, be the sun and shine on your garden. With love and perseverance. And it will grow. It is OK to be nonconformist. If you didn't shine at school, or take kindly, or easily, to becoming a multi skilled all rounder, all is not lost. You may just have exactly what it takes to become an outstanding entrepreneur.

## 11. THE ABILITY TO FAIL

Above all else, you need to have the ability to fail, the ability to have ideas and sell those ideas, the courage to execute those ideas, and be persistent enough to wear away mountains—so that, if you fail, you learn and move on to the next adventure, to the next dream. This is a 180 degree change of mindset from employment. Nurturing ideas is an ability which grows fast with practice. Ideas don't have to be only business ideas. They can also include ideas which can help you escape from tricky situations.

You need to do all this—and then you need to take the word 'fail' out of your vocabulary. Everything we do in life is a success. We breathe. We love. We practise kindness. We deal with other human beings. We have experiences. We improve. This is magnificent and abundant success.

### III. OPENNESS TO IDEAS

Be an ideas machine. Come up with ten new ideas every day. No, that was not a typo. I did say EVERY day. By doing that you will exercise your ideas muscle. Many of the ten ideas will be impracticable and will never grow in the sunshine. List them anyway. Some will. By doing this, daily, you will reach the point, in a few weeks, where you are brimming with new ideas. And new ideas are the air which entrepreneurs breathe. Ideas are the currency of life, more than money, because while money can run out, good ideas never do. Good ideas buy you good experiences and more time. They can even save your life.

### IV. BALANCE OPTIMISM WITH DISAPPOINTMENT

'Prepare for the worst, hope for the best, and expect something in the middle'. Try to walk the line between pessimism and over optimism. Not a bad mantra for the entrepreneur. On the entrepreneurial journey there will be unseen, unfamiliar and unexpected obstacles to be circumnavigated. There will be disappointments. There will be difficult, sometimes impossible, people to deal with. There will be mistakes, many of them your own, some of them expensive. There will be moments where tough decisions need to be taken. There will be times when over optimism is punished, where crisis management is needed as a band-aid because of a lack of proper planning, where people let you down, where teams make mistakes through lack of joined up thinking, where inattention to detail is expensive, where there is a downturn in the market, when a competitor damages your business, where a failure to implement results in a missed opportunity, where greed steps in and you forget your principles for a moment, where there is too much pressure and something is overlooked, when you get the experience which comes from not getting what you want. What a list. I'm sure you know all of that. And yet you still want to set up a business. That's optimism. That's hope. And the entrepreneur runs out of fuel without those two. List your achievements and review them regularly. They are a wonderful way of topping up that fuel tank.

v. **RESILIENCE AND COURAGE**
When you have been an entrepreneur for a few years, you may have to pick yourself up, dust yourself off, and start all over again. To do that you have to develop almost super human resilience. You will need courage—that's moral courage—to state your truth, fairly and squarely, whenever it needs to be stated. To be firm in any decision you take and considerate in how you carry it out. To always implement your decisions, without vacillating. And without fear or favour.

VI. **LOVE**

Yes, the L-word. Love for your business. Love for your team. Love for your clients and customers. Love for all those around you, who remind you not to sacrifice quality of life with them for work, work, work. And love for yourself. You must become a true networker and connector—nurturing a love of people with a desire to help them, even ahead of your own advancement. This will make a huge difference to your success. And just remember this. Life is not a portfolio—neither for a start up founder, nor for anyone else. An entrepreneur cannot diversify—at least until he, or she, has a business which is fully established and robust. He or she cannot keep dozens of options open at all times. So, love your business, focus on it, and love your people too. That will give you the best chance of prospering.

# The Growing Process

Let's return to this idea of untangling the Technician, the Manager and the Entrepreneur. As I have said, it can lead to conflicts. So how do these conflicts get resolved? With time, and awareness, and a commitment to learn and evolve. Because each of those three roles serve you, at each stage of your business, as you get it off the ground.

Consider those phases here, as a parallel with a young child growing into adulthood.

In its Infant phase, the Technician is in charge —working all hours that God made. Technicians learn to be master jugglers. They get early success, but then, inevitably, they drop behind. There are rows at home. They cannot keep up. They're great as technicians, but useless as business owners. And they don't have time to manage. They see the world from the bottom up, from a tactical viewpoint not a strategic viewpoint. The business depends on them, and when a business depends on someone, that someone does not have a business, they have a job. The Infancy stage of a business is easy to spot, because the owner and the business are effectively one and the same. When the owner is doing what he or she wants to do, not what the business needs…

The Adolescent stage comes when the business owner decides it's time to get some help—usually precipitated by an Infancy crisis. You might go out and get technical help. A sales-orientated owner goes for production help, and vice versa. They hit the 'I don't have to do that any more' moment. The new hire is a blessing at first. You give them free rein. You don't have time to supervise them. You get into management by abdication. The new unmanaged hire starts to drop balls. The hire has to go. You go back to being the technician again. You cannot see any other way, because you just proved any other way doesn't work.

The MATURE phase only comes when you move outside your comfort zone and see that you must play the Entrepreneur; the Manager must play the manager; and the Technician must play the technician. It comes when the Entrepreneur envisages the business as something separate from themselves—when they answer the dreaming question: 'Why this business, and not that business?'. A mature business is essentially very different to the business in which you worked as a technician.

So, there you have it. The big conundrum facing all start-up businesses. The main reason why they fail in droves. This is a crying shame, for those who lead small-to-medium sized enterprises are the unspoken heroes of our economy, and they deserve far more nurturing and support than they currently get. If only someone could whisper in their ear at the start.

But all is not lost. There is a solution.

# CHAPTER TWO

# FLIGHT SCHOOL

From the very beginning, it is essential to see the start-up you are building as something separate from you. It is not, as some see it at first, your life, your whole existence. Neither is it just a job; another 9 to 5. It exists somewhere in the middle. It is an entity you build that should, in time, have an entirely separate life from yours. You might hang on to it, keep it in your family, or you might sell it. In time. For now, from day one, you need to think of it as a building, and yourself as its architect. You are not, and never can be, the actual building.

Excited about your vision, you think about the interior design of the building, how it will look and feel. But before all that, you need the plans. The dimensions. The materials list. The budget. The timings. Surprisingly, that's the bit that many entrepreneurs fail to put in place. If these details are not ironed out at the start, the chances of failure increase exponentially. There will be no solid foundations for the business to be built on. This, coupled with the war between the Technician, Manager and Entrepreneur, outlined in the last chapter, is another huge reason why survival rates are so low.

To return to the aviation metaphor: you can see yourself in the cockpit. You know the places you want to go to. But before all of that comes flight school—the essential thinking and training that must come before you're ready to lift off.

# The Kipling Questions

Flight school begins with answering six questions, once posed by Rudyard Kipling:

> 'I keep six serving men;
> They taught me all I knew:
> Their names are What, and Why and When; and
> How and Where and Who.'

Just as they served Kipling, they serve every entrepreneur. They lead, very often, to blindingly obvious solutions, but common sense is not always common practice. Work through these questions. Take time on it. These are your foundations, essential if your building is to be strong. You will also find them on a worksheet at the end of this book.

You must study the end game before everything else, because long term planning is so often undervalued in our indefinite short term world:

**WHAT**—These are the hardest questions so I have tried to help with the answers.

- What business are you setting up? *Think hard about your choice. You can waste a lot of time barking up the wrong tree;*
- What will it sell? *Once you have established the outline of the product or service, you need to drill down, in much detail, into the specifics;*
- What are your strong skills? *Ask yourself, and ask others. Knowing yourself is of vital importance;*
- What are you less good at? *Be tough on yourself. Others will tell you if you are honest enough to ask them;*
- What do you want out of it? *What effect will it have on your life?*
- What will you do with it when it is built? *Here, you need really deep thought. Imagine it is fully developed now. Are you going to keep it? Or sell it? Get someone else to manage it?*
- What are the skills of the rest of the team? Are they complementary or duplicates? *The answers to this question will come more easily once you have completed your own skills audit;*
- What do you need to take out of it while you are building it? *This will help you when preparing cashflows. Be aware of one thing—if you are trying to attract others' investment, they will expect your drawings to be modest during the early stages.*

**WHY**—**Why are you setting it up?**
- To give you a strong financial future?
- As an interesting sideline?
- To grow and then sell?
- To keep in the family?

**WHEN**
- When are you going to start it?
- When will it be built?
- When will you hire others to help you?
- When will it be 'finished'—ready to keep or sell?

**How**
- How are you going to build it? *On your own, with others, over what period of time?*
- How are you going to finance it? *With your own money, with money from friends and family? With loans? Or a mixture of the above, as is so often the case?*

**WHERE**
- Where are you going to operate from? *Home, an existing or new office?*
- Where are you going to source your products, services? *At this point, you should be going into a lot of detail here.*
- Where will you find customers and clients? *Make sure they exist. Do some market research. Do not assume.*

## Who

- Who is the Entrepreneur? *Big question. Is that you? Or do you just think it is?*
- Who is the Technician? *Same question as the above.*
- Who will be your team? *If you do not yet know the names of the team, you must, by this stage, understand the skills you are looking for;*
- Who else is going to be working with you? *See my question about your team above;*
- Who is the Manager? *Same question as the above. You must be able to identify Entrepreneur, Technician & Manager. If you cannot, your start will be very bumpy;*
- Who will you get to advise you—both on business strategy and on finance? *This is a massively important question. You need to have a handle on the numbers—budgeted numbers and actual numbers—at all times. Lose sight of these and I promise you, from bitter experience, that you will regret it.*

These are just the beginnings of a whole range of questions which must be asked, and answered, before you can start to build any serious business. More questions will come as you read this book.

# Identifying Stuckness

We all get stuck from time to time, and business is somewhere where it is all too easy to get stuck. The places where we get stuck may well differ, but my guess would be that they fall into one or more of the areas below:

- Are you a broad brush or detail person?
- Are you a starter or a finisher? Or, ideally, both?
- Are you good at getting things going? Or, better at finishing them off?
- Will you allow yourself to feel fear, while still managing it, so you become braver all the time?
- Have you got what you need to be an entrepreneur?
- What is the big idea for your product or service?
- What is the plan for your business? Do you know where you are now and where you want to be in three years?
- Are you managing your finances? Are your costs under control? Is your pricing right?
- Are you good at dealing with people? Have you got the right mix of skills? The right advisors?
- Are you happy with your branding and marketing? With the way in which your offering is presented?
- Are you happy with how sales and prospecting are going? With the building of your pipeline?
- How are you getting on with creating systems

and processes? Have you got these in place?
- How is your networking? How good are your contacts? Are you a connector?
- Are you a good negotiator?
- Does your thinking need refreshing?
- How will you develop the business further? And in what ways?
- How will you deal with succession?
- How are you going to reboot, reorganise or rescue the business? And if all else fails, how do you plan to start again?

Work through this list for yourself. Be brutally honest. At any one time, even in successful and established businesses, at least one or more of these things will be in need of attention and correction. Honesty is the key here. Think honestly, act quickly, learn, adapt and change. Your business has to be agile if it's going to survive, let alone grow. Your honesty will become one of its surest protectors.

# Seven Essential Things

I have found that there are seven things that EVERY business needs, and another three that some businesses need.

- **THE ESSENTIALS**
1. A three to five year plan, broken down into quarters;
2. A real time financial dashboard;
3. A strong team—and regular, properly run, meetings;
4. A clear direction and focus, with systems to leverage time effectively;
5. A regular blue sky thinking session;
6. A marketing and communications strategy and programme; &
7. A Trusted Advisor or Critical Friend.

Most businesses have only a few of these in place—at best—and many will not be functioning to capacity. In addition, some businesses also need to have:

1. A start-up, or early stage, plan in place;
2. Help to manage changes of ownership—buy outs or buy ins, straight sales, changes of partner(s); and
3. Advice on how to deal with reorganising, rebooting or restructuring the business.

# Some Tips

As you read on, I hope that *Lift Off!* will help you to un-pick the maze that is entrepreneurship, knock a number of myths on the head, and reduce the stress and anxiety which is so often, quite unnecessarily, present in the day to day affairs of every small business. In the meantime, here are some practical ways to make sure you approach business with the right mindset…

- **THEMES NOT LISTS**
  Create themes in your life, and live by them, not by to-do lists. To-do lists regiment us, bring us stress and lead us into slavery. If we concentrate on the practice of growing ourselves just one per cent phys-ically, spirituality, mentally and emotionally every day, themes will suggest themselves and start to guide our lives in much better directions.

- **21 DAY HABIT TRAINING**
  You will need to commit to good thinking, and good working, habits, while rejecting less helpful habits. In my view, if you pursue the acquisition of a new habit, it will take you about 21 days to cement it firmly into the way in which you do things. In other words, at the end of that period, it should be easier for you to do it than not to do it.

- **SAYING NO**

  You need to learn to say 'no'. It is easier to say 'yes'. But, if you say 'no' sometimes, you are in better control of your time, and, thus, of your life. Try this— here are my rules to decide if I should say 'yes' or 'no'. Two out of the three questions below need to be answered 'yes' for me not to say 'no' to the request, project, whatever it is:

  o   Will I learn something new?
  o   Will it be fun?
  o   Will it be worthwhile financially?

  In this context, remember not to chase every deal. Have enough deals in your pipeline so you don't have to. This is just so important. It takes time to learn which ones are worth devoting time to, and those to avoid. It's just so easy, in business as in life, to get involved in time wasting activities which result in no long term gain to us. And meantime, the time we have devoted to them has slipped, forever, like sand through a timer.

- **... BUT NOT ALWAYS LISTENING TO THE NOS OF OTHERS**

  You will need to learn to be aware of the doomsayers. The enemies of small business.

Many of whom are just around the corner. They are likely to include members of your family, your friends, maybe your bank, quite possibly your accountant. They will try to blow you off course, often for good reasons of their own, sometimes for the wrong reasons, usually through some lack of understanding of what it is you are trying to do. Avoid negative people like the plague—run from them as fast as your feet will carry you.

- **THINK IN QUADRANTS**
Among all the conflicting pressures on you, you will need to keep things simple, taking small steps rather than getting lost in massive initiatives. You will need to plan using time management tools that work for you—whether those are notes, reminders, timetables or whatever works best—making sure not to fritter time on pointless calls, emails or meetings—keeping a 'door ajar rather than door open' policy can help with the latter.

In Stephen Covey's book *The Seven Habits of Highly Effective People*, he talks about four Quadrants:

1. Urgent and important (your own crises);
2. Important but not urgent (planning time);
3. Urgent but not important (other people's crises); and

4.  Neither important nor urgent (time wasting tasks with no real benefit).

Covey tells us to spend more and more time in quadrant 2, which will eventually cause quadrant 1 to shrink, to pay scant regard to quadrant 3 and to ignore quadrant 4 altogether. If you find piles of reading building up, put them in a briefcase to read when you are waiting before meetings, on a train and so on.

You will need to block out time or it fills up with dross. Working a straight three hours in the morning, and likewise in the afternoon, can be a lot more effective—cutting slack for breaks—than just ploughing on for the standard eight hours— or even longer. Don't be a busy fool. KISS or *Keep It Simple, Stupid*. Learn to be fleet of foot, to multi task, and to think ahead...

- **AVOID THE 9 DISTRACTIONS**
    In the Yoga Sutras poem, written in about 300AD, there is a line about the obstacles we encounter in yoga. These obstacles are distractions caused by:

    o   CARELESSNESS
    o   CRAVING
    o   DELUSION

- ○ DISEASE
- ○ DOUBT
- ○ DULLNESS
- ○ LAZINESS
- ○ NOT ACHIEVING DESIRED OBJECTIVES, and
- ○ UNSTEADINESS

They were written, centuries ago, about yoga, but they could just as easily be applied, today, to the pursuit of entrepreneurship.

- **LOOK AFTER NUMBER ONE**
  1. Focus on eight hours sleep a night—this should be at the very top of your list. The gap between despair and hope is usually bridged by a good night's sleep. Sleep should be followed by…
  2. Never doing Stress (pressure is fine, but stress is absolutely not). Don't hallucinate or nurture worries through tiredness, or an overactive imagination, and..
  3. Focus on a healthy Diet, and then…
  4. Take light Exercise.

Those four things: Sleep, no Stress, Diet and Exercise—in that order—will make a massive difference to your performance. To keep control of yourself, try, every day, to focus on routine, on your fitness, on doing something creative—and, keep a diary.

Practising daily will make you very good—because you will get a little bit better every single day. Self discipline is critical: when things get tough, this must kick in, and it will kick in a lot more effectively if it has been learned, and practised, in easier times. And, make sure you tell yourself positive stories, which will make it far easier for you to get into flow and play at the top of your game.

# CHAPTER THREE

# ARE YOU IN THE RIGHT AIRCRAFT?

Tell me about your business. About what motivated you to start it. Fire me up. Be sure you are excited. Because you are going to have to excite others with it too. So, start by exciting me.

Chances are, if you're reading this book, you have a pretty good idea of what your business is. Some of you may already be up and selling. Some of you may not. Deciding what to sell is, in some ways, the hardest part. *So many things have been done,* you might say. *There are so few ideas left.* Those worries could have been written at any time in history, and they would be just as untrue now as they were then. The level of invention, in the UK alone, has probably never been higher. With the internet, this is ever truer. There are ALWAYS new products or services to be created, or new ways out there to alter existing products or deliver existing services in new ways. We live in exciting times. Perhaps some of the most exciting times in business. Ever.

Remember this too: your product or service is NOT the only one in the world. You may find yourself held in a vice-like grip by your excitement about it, just as we are when we fall in love. Your passion and enthusiasm can drive you beyond common sense. This is where it helps to have alongside you an advisor, or 'critical friend', to put you back in your box, on occasions. Watch some back episodes of *Dragon's Den* to remind you why this is so important.

## Are You in The Right Aircraft?

Whether you've launched your business or not, these key questions below must be asked. It's possible to be a gifted pilot, an intuitive navigator, and still be in the wrong kind of plane.

- Is it scalable?
- Are the local demographics favourable to you? I mean, if you set up the only dry cleaner in a local town, you are likely to do well. If there are ten others…what then?
- Have you a brand in mind? Have you worked on it? Asked people what they think of it? Is it visually strong, catchy, memorable?
- Could you see it attracting a big network of support?
- Better still, could you be creating a monopoly—

even if only a local one? The only ferry to the island?

Also, might your product or service be of any use in the five human situations below—generally known as the five Ds:

- DEATH?
- DEBT?
- DELAY?
- DESPERATION?
- DIVORCE?

More generally:

- What does your competition consist of?
- How do their offerings compare to yours?
- Are your offerings well structured?
- Have you split them into different levels— from entry to premium?
- Are your offerings clearly distinguished from those of the competition?
- How does your pricing compare with theirs?
- What's so special about your offering as against theirs?
- How big a market are you selling into?
- How are you finding your customers?
- How well funded are they?

- How well funded are you?
- How seasonal is your offering?
- How long a shelf life has your offering?

If your offering is of a product rather than a service, you might add in:

- How good are your margins?
- Where do you manufacture your product?
- How easily can it be produced?
- How many could you sell in the first three years?
- How much stock would you need to hold?

And from there, more questions will suggest themselves. Be honest with yourself and your business. If you're not in the right aircraft, your chances of a crash landing become exponentially greater.

## Is That Aircraft Fit to Fly?

If you have ever watched any episodes of either *The Apprentice* or *Dragon's Den*, you will be aware how business ideas get tested by experienced businessmen and women, and how an apparently well-designed business idea can be quickly turned into dust under intense scrutiny. However, while we often see good people on those shows, who many of us would love to have working for us or alongside us, it is, for me at least, very hard to find a robust business idea among them. One which is scalable, shows a good margin, and is not likely to be killed off by larger competition.

Most of the time we listen to business pitches from people who do not have a proper grip on their figures, who have not thought through the potential risks and threats to their business, or who have failed to see that their business is completely unscalable and is therefore unattractive to investors. And yet they appear willing to put, or have already put, a major chunk of their life savings into the project. At the same time as asking for investment based on a completely unrealistic valuation.

What is sad about this is that, had they had a mentor with any real world entrepreneurial experience, who they had asked about their idea and their funding plan before committing to it, they might have been advised to approach it in a different way, or possibly abandon it altogether. But, sadly, there are very few around who are qualified to provide such utterly vital advice. And the only ones who can help here are those who have been tested in the fires of business themselves.

Here are some more rather critical questions which might be included among those that should be asked by a would-be entrepreneur considering a start-up:

- What are the strengths of the product or service?
- If appropriate, is it patented?
- What are its weaknesses?
- What opportunities does it bring?
- What threats are linked to it?
- How unique is it?
- What is the quality of it? (a lot more important than its price).
- Is anything similar on offer? And, at what price? And, is it succeeding?
- How well received has it been?
- How big is the demand?
- How good are the margins?
- How fashionable/seasonal is it?
- How much capital is it likely to take to promote it?
- What size premises would you need?
- What staffing would you need?
- What equipment would you need?
- Where are you going to get the money, if needed, and on what terms?

The questions go on and on, and you have to keep drilling down until you start to understand your business forensically. And only when you get to the end of those questions, can you possibly tell whether yours is a venture that is worth taking forward.

This is the stage where you need to put in very considerable head time. It is hard work, which everyone would prefer to avoid, but it can get very expensive if you fail to do it and do it now.

I have said this before, but it is so important that I am going to repeat it. You now have to decide how excited you are about your offering. Do you wake up and think about it in the night? Can you see it delivering everything you dream for it in the coming years? If it is igniting your passion, there's a good chance you may be able to ignite other people to get behind it as well.

But, if it isn't, you should think very carefully before proceeding with it. Check that the market is attractive, the business and the proposition are sustainable, the offering is scalable and capable of execution.

## The Test Flight

You have your aircraft. You've done your training. Are you ready to take it for a spin? One test flight will tell you if your aircraft is airworthy. Same in your business. So how do we test it?

Ted Nicholas, the American direct mail guru, once told me that he liked to 'shoot his fish in the bucket'. What he meant by that was that he liked to test everything, which of course you could do then with direct mail, just as you now can with the internet. He would 'test small and roll out big' when a piece of copy worked. With the internet, the same is possible, so it seems madness not to test a product or service, both online and offline, with trusted people we know, as well as with people we don't know, so as to give us the best possible chance of success—either by abandoning the offering altogether, or modifying it.

# The Elevator Pitch

Assuming that we have done this, and we go on to make it our business and launch it, then we should know EVERYTHING there is to know about EVERY benefit of our offering, and be able to present what is known as an 'Elevator Pitch' to anyone who shows any interest.

What is meant by an elevator pitch is essentially what you would say to someone if you were travelling up four floors with them in a lift and wanted to attract their investment. You'd have to be very brief, very pithy, focused on the benefits of the offering, clear on what investors would get, to stand any chance of piquing their interest.

There are no hard and fast rules as to how to construct an elevator pitch, but to create a really excellent one, start by summarising the benefits and USP(s) of your business on one page. Now edit that page into 150 words. Now cut it back to one long sentence. Test it on a couple of people whose opinions you trust. Make sure that it answers all the questions that a seasoned investor might ask. Or, leaves you prepared to do so, when they get asked. Now try it again as a pitch and keep honing it until it becomes second nature to you. You are now ready to get into that lift.

And when it comes to delivering your pitch, practise practise practise, and follow these rules:

- Dress smartly
- Smile
- Be friendly
- Be empathetic—get the party you are pitching to on side
- Relate to your opposite number
- Laugh
- Listen
- Ask questions
- Share your joy in finding a fellow traveller

You have 30 seconds to pitch the classic 'elevator pitch.'

I've been scared and desperate and afraid to ask someone to give me, want me, love me, all in the space of a short lift ride.

The ideas below have worked for me.

- **WHO ARE YOU?**
  People want to know they are talking to a good, honest, reliable person who they can trust and perhaps even like, or love. Yes, love—that was not a misprint.

They won't love you by looking at your CV.

You have to do method acting. Imagine what your body would feel like if they'd already said 'yes' even before you opened your mouth.

You would be standing up straight, smiling, palms open, ready to close the deal. You have to method act at the beginning of your pitch.

If you are slouched, then your brain is not as well connected to your nervous system and you won't be in 'flow'. Also, you will look untrustworthy.

- **Relax**
  Think about how you breathe when you are anxious and nervous. I will tell you how I breathe: short, shallow breaths in my upper chest. So, do the reverse before you pitch.

  Breathe deep and in your stomach. Even three deep breaths in the stomach has been shown to totally relax the mind and body. People sense this. Again, this builds trust and relaxes you.

- **Yeah. Uh. Um….**
  I have a hard time with this. It seems natural to say 'yup' or 'right' or 'uh' or whatever. But here are the

facts — people perceive you as stupid when you do this.

Just keep quiet when someone is talking. Then, when the other person has finished speaking, wait for two seconds before responding. They might not be done yet. And it gives you time to think of a response. If you are thinking of a response, while they are talking, then you aren't listening to them.

People unconsciously know when you are not listening to them. Then they say no to you.

· **THE FOUR U'S**
Finally, now, we're getting to the heart of the matter.

Here are the four U's.

They give you a way to consolidate your vision into a sentence or two—and then express it in a clear manner.

Think about these things when talking:

1. URGENCY. Why the problem you solve is urgent to your demographic. For example: 'I can never get a taxi when it rains!'
2. UNIQUE. Why your solution is unique:

'We aggregate 100s of car services into one simple app. Nobody else does this.'

3.   USEFUL. Why your solution is useful to the lives of the people you plan on selling to: 'We get you there on time.'

4.   ULTRA-SPECIFIC. This shows there is no fluff: 'Our app knows where you are. Your credit card is pre-loaded. You hit a button and a car shows up in 4-5 minutes'.

Here is a fifth bonus U:

5.   USER-FRIENDLY. In other words, make it as easy as possible for someone to say yes. Like a money-back guarantee, for instance.

Oh, and before I forget it, a sixth U:

6.   UNQUESTIONABLE PROOF. This can be in the form of profits. Or some other measurable statistic. Or testimonials. Whatever it takes.

- DESIRE

A lot of people say you have to satisfy the desires of the other person in order for them to say yes. As much as we would like to think otherwise, people primarily act out of self-interest.

The less they know you, the more they will act out of self-interest because to do otherwise could potentially put them in danger. We all know that kids shouldn't take sweets from strangers.

In an elevator pitch, the investor is the kid, what you are asking for are the sweets, and you are the stranger. So, their gut reflex, unless you make the sweets super sweet, is to say 'no'.

So, what are their desires? They are will usually include a mix of the following:

○ RECOGNITION
○ REJUVENATION
○ RELAXATION
○ RELIEF
○ RELIGION
○ REMUNERATION
○ RESULTS
○ REVENGE, and
○ ROMANCE

If you can help them solve these URGENT problems or desires, then they are more likely to say 'yes' to you.

I don't know what you are selling, but hopefully it's not to satisfy their desire for revenge. But if it is, don't do anything violent!

- **OBJECTIONS**

  Everyone is going to have gut objections. They've been approached 1,000s of times before.

  I'll provide solutions to these objections:

  ○ No TIME. That's OK. It's on a lift. So, they have lift-length time. The key here is to stand straight and act like someone who deserves to be listened to.
  ○ No INTEREST. You solve this by accurately expressing the urgency of the problem.
  ○ No PERCEIVED DIFFERENCE. But you have your unique difference ready to go.
  ○ No BELIEF. Offer unquestionable proof that this works.
  ○ No DECISION. Make their decision as user-friendly as possible.

With great power comes great responsibility.

Most people don't have the power of persuasion. They mess up on each of the points I've outlined above. It takes practice and hard work.But this is not just about persuasion. It's about connection.

It's about two people, who are probably strangers, reaching through physical and mental space and trying to understand each other and reach common ground. It's not about money. It's not about the idea. It's not about yes or no.

You'll probably think I have gone too far here, but, it is actually about two people falling in love.

This is all about the power of asking. If you don't ask, the answer is always no. You miss all the shots you don't take. So, why not just do your prep, brave up, and ask? You either win, or you learn.

If you get those things right, the pitch will go well. But, remember not to be a time thief—be precise and pithy. That should be easy, because, by now, you have done your practising. There's no guarantee that the person you are pitching to will buy you (and, be in no doubt, they MUST buy you before they buy your business) but, if you don't do these things, they most definitely won't. Test your offerings, on a small basis, with a trusted crowd. Get those people to be very honest. Make changes as needed. Test that offering again. And again. If it works, you will then, and only then, have the confidence to roll it out— slowly at first, faster later...

# The Critical Friend

I have said this before, but it's worth saying it again: find somebody who can become your trusted advisor and critical friend while you go through this process. Start-ups are lean places, where there's usually not a lot of money around, but it is surely worth spending a little of it, early on, on wise advice as an alternative to risking losing your shirt if you have not built your house on sound foundations. Or, give that person a few shares if you prefer.

Really think around your offering. Think of ways to get prospective customers to buy your goods and services through an attractive starter deal—something that is really good value and gives them confidence in your company—before they feel they trust you, and are therefore ready to spend more with you on higher value goods and services. This area deserves deep consideration.

# Buying Someone Else's Aircraft

There is an alternative here to taking a new aircraft out for a test flight, and that is buying someone else's aircraft: buying a business rather than starting one. There are a number of advantages to this, including that it is ready to fly, and you don't, perhaps surprisingly, always need vast amounts of money to acquire it. The diagnostic questions remain the same, and you need to put the same thought, planning and other considerations into place before you even consider taking off in it. Deep due diligence is vital in this area.

CHAPTER FOUR

# THE FLIGHT PLAN

Pilot training? Check. Right aircraft? Check. Ready to head for the skies? Not quite yet. You might crash without a clear flight plan. Without knowing where to go. And without having it clearly and concisely written down. It is truly astonishing how rarely critical life-changing goals are written down. It is almost as if they weren't worth achieving. But there are two reasons why most people fail to commit them to paper. The first is the fear that they might sound too grandiose, too un-realistic, too unachievable. Thus, that they might not be achieved. That their non-achievement might diminish the author for being a dreamer. The second comes from a lack of understanding of the superpower that flows from written goals.

The importance of a written goal, which reflects the passionate desires of its author, cannot be overstated when it comes to delivering on those desires. It provides clarity of direction. It sets out the timetable for arrival. It is watered by the author's continuous visualisation of its desirable outcome.

In this chapter we will apply such a crucial step to your business. You might think you've already done that. But read on. Entrepreneurs are, by their nature, creators and dreamers. Often difficult, uncompromising and perhaps impossible at times (Elon Musk comes to mind here), we all start with big dreams that must be committed to paper—in both long, and later, short form—so they can be shared with others, either in the form of elevator pitches or longer working documents.

## Goethe's Providence

Johann Wolfgang von Goethe was born in 1749. A German poet, playwright, novelist, scientist, statesman, theatre director, critic, and amateur artist, he is often considered the greatest German literary figure of the modern era. He was well ahead of his time. He wrote this:

> 'Until one is committed, there is hesitancy, the chance to draw back, always ineffectiveness. Concerning all acts of initiative and creation, there is one elementary truth, the ignorance of which kills countless ideas and splendid plans: that the moment one definitely commits oneself, then Providence moves too.'

Call it what you will—serendipity perhaps—but if you set out your goals in faith that they will be achieved, then 'Providence' will follow.

Perhaps this sounds a bit woolly for a business book, but, let me assure you that it is not. We are told to write business plans, whatever those might be. These are usually dry, unrealistic, number-heavy proposals, generally destined to be read (or not) by potential bankers and/or investors. They usually bore the life out of the writer, and, therefore, unsurprisingly, the audience as well. Because of the way they are constructed, they stifle both the dreams of the writer and, thereby, any possible enthusiasm by the reader.

I am perhaps being a little unkind. But only a little. Such documents *do* have their place. But that place is not the place of goal setting. Think of any of the great entrepreneurs of our age. We all have our own favourites, I am sure, but mine would include the late Jimmy Goldsmith, James Dyson, Richard Branson, Anthony Bamford, Alan Sugar, Luke Johnson, Elon Musk and the late lamented Tom Watson (of IBM).

When Tom Watson started IBM, he set out his vision of how he was going to build the company into what it turned out to be. It is worth reading this vision in full. There is a lot we can learn from it. Note my highlights in bold:

'IBM is what it is today for three special reasons. The first reason is that, at the very beginning, **I had a very clear picture of what the company would**

**look like when it was finally done.** You might say I had a model in my mind of what it would look like when the dream—my vision—was in place. The second reason was that once I had that picture, **I then asked myself how a company, which looked like that, would have to act.** I then created a picture of how IBM would act when it was finally done.

The third reason IBM has been so successful was that once I had a picture of how IBM would look when the dream was in place, and how such a company would have to act, I then realised that, unless we began to act that way from the very beginning, we would never get there. In other words, **I realised that for IBM to become a great company it would have to act like a great company long before it ever became one.**

From the very outset, IBM was fashioned after the template of my vision. And each, and every, day we attempted to model the company after that template. At the end of each day, we asked ourselves how well we had done, discovered the disparity between where we were and where we had committed ourselves to be, and, at the start of the following day, set out to make up for the difference. Every day at IBM was a day devoted to business development, not doing business. **We didn't do business at IBM, we built one.'**

It would be difficult, if not impossible, to put the mission we all need to achieve in our businesses better than Tom Watson does here. Try this for your business:

- What will your company look like?
- How would that vision of a company need to act?
- How can you act that way from the beginning?

## Three Years and Twelve Quarters

When you set goals, you've got to be specific. You've got to know exactly what your destination is. You've got to have a burning desire to get there. Got to believe you are going to get there. Know that you are going to get there.

So, back to business, you need to set goals for the next three years. You need to ask some very penetrating questions, so as to obtain detailed answers about revenues, about costs, about profitability, about the team. And then you have to add the dream because, like Tom Watson, you are only going to get to where you want to be in three years if you can build that dream. And know what you are going to do with it when you have done so.

Then, you've got to work back, quarter by quarter, from the twelfth quarter, the one which completes the three years, to the quarter you are in now, as you stand at the start of the journey. That plan has got to include every element of the business—products or services, marketing, finance, the team, systems, etc. And, like Tom Watson, you have got to build the path to your destination.

This is tough work. Thinking is the hardest work we ever have to do. And we will make endless excuses to put it off. So, don't, because doing it here, in this way, will give you the ticket to everything you want from your business. And, not doing so, will consign you to not having it.

Why three years? Because five is too long to visualise, and one is too short for a plan. Three gives you the perspective and time to smooth out inevitable peaks and troughs. Also, three years consists of just twelve quarters. If you want, you can create a three-year rolling programme, and keep adding an extra year on to the end, when you finish the last one.

While you are creating this three-year plan—which should be stimulating and fun—you need to focus on deciding three things:

- What the business will look like when it is done
- When it will be done
- What you are going to do with it once it is done

It is quite impossible to overstress how vital it is to come up with the answers to these three questions, from the outset.

Arguably, the third decision is the hardest. You must decide whether you are going to hang on to it, or whether you intend to sell it. And you must decide, as Tom Watson did, to build a big business, that others will want to buy, while remembering that you are a small business just for now.

Walt Disney died before the Epcot Centre was finished. Epcot was Walt's dream. Others continued to work on it after he died, and eventually it was finished. Walt's brother, Roy, was showing an important colleague of Walt's around the finished centre. 'What a pity Walt never saw this,' the visitor said. Roy replied, 'Well, if he hadn't, we wouldn't be here now'.

The power of visualisation is incredibly strong, because, through it, we are building our 'future histories'—a powerful phrase, used by Mohammed Ali when he famously lost to Joe Frazier in 1971. Interviewed afterwards, Ali simply reflected: 'That day, he had a stronger future history than me.'

## Taking it Step by Step

Goethe had it right when he said that when there is commitment 'Providence moves too'. The power of direction and focus makes any endeavour so much more unstoppable than one where these are not in place. Setting objectives, and targets, as subsets of such an overall plan, breaks it all down into digestible and much more achievable chunks.

Three years may seem like a long time; thus the importance of slicing it down into quarters, of which there are only twelve in that period. Each quarter creates its own smaller time frame—a place where pieces of the three-year jigsaw can be put, or at least provisionally parked, while the overall plan is honed and revised. We can break the current quarter down into months, weeks and days—even into the granularity of the school timetable—mornings, afternoons and even hours. Three months isn't very long.

The principle to follow here is that the plan is intended to be a map of our mountain climb—it takes us from the valley floor, through the foothills, up to base camp. From there we walk up some slightly steeper slopes, to camp one. After that, things start to get a little more serious and grown up—we might need to be roped together in places, the terrain a little less predictable, the weather a little colder.

We get to camp two, rest, check our provisions—crampons on, fully roped up now, with the occasional need for ladders or ice axes—we continue to camp three, testing all that we have learned up to this point. From there, the conditions get colder, the weather less predictable, the ground steeper. Rested, we press on to camp four.

We are now fired up for the summit. We rise early, check the weather forecast, decide when to leave. Roped again, and using oxygen, we start out for the big one. And, just like that, when we have set out our plan, it becomes a living document—absolutely not a thing to put in a drawer to gather dust. Remember Tom Watson and follow his example.

If we have elements that we don't fully understand, and there will be some, we can park them in a later quarter—approximately when we think they might fall into place—and leave them to review again a little further down the road.

I am going to finish this chapter with a silly little story. One sunny day, there were three frogs sitting on lily pads floating lazily down a river. Some way ahead lay a weir. The frogs were all unaware. Just enjoying the journey. But, then, two of the frogs decided to get off their lily pads. The river flowed on. Eventually the lily pads floated to the edge of the weir, where the water frothed and bubbled, and all got washed over the edge.

I have a question for you. How many frogs went over the weir?

'Well, just the one that didn't get off,' I hear you say. It's a reasonable answer, but it's the wrong one. In fact, all three got washed over the weir and perished in the maelstrom of churning water below.

'But you said that two of the frogs got off,' you protest.

I didn't say that. I said they decided to get off... but then THEY DID NOTHING ABOUT IT and thus drowned. That's the very silly story that I promised you, but one, which, I believe aptly illustrates the dangers of inaction and lack of implementation. So, when you come to creating your business plan, please, for your sake, don't behave like those frogs. Just do it. If you fail to do it, you will have only yourself to blame.

CHAPTER FIVE

# FUELLING UP

If you think back to the Introduction, where I first posed this metaphor of flying, you'll remember that the fuel was the cash every business needs. The importance of the production of cashflows cannot be overstated. Firstly, there will be the injection of grubstakes to get the business going, usually from friends and family, with further rounds of investment as time goes on.

It is vital that this cash is subject to very careful husbandry, so that it is not wasted, which is why cashflows form such a vital part in the provision of the overall budgets. If you still have cash, you're still in business. If you run out, you have to stop. Thus, intense focus on cash, at all times, is compulsory rather than optional. Because running out of fuel can have disastrous—usually terminal—consequences.

It's interesting to me, when we have so much focus on money, that we usually fail to understand important questions around its psychology. It isn't a simple case of numbers going up or down. Wealth is as much about wellbeing as anything else. It's not just about piles of cold money. It's about our families, our homes, our health, our friends, our leisure, our community—as well as our career, and finance itself.

Would you drive a car at speed, in the dark, without your headlights on? If the answer is yes, you'll need more than this book to help you. But, even if you would not do that, you would be in good company if you tried to run your business with a financial blindfold on. Because that is exactly what most small businesses do. Another reason why so many of them fail.

Thinking about money boils down to three key things: making it, keeping it and growing it. All of those things need learning. We also have to decide if we want to be broke, comfortable or rich. And if that sounds oversimplified, it's because humans tend to over-complicate.

We usually aren't taught how to be comfortable and smart with money from a young age. As a result, through an absence of understanding of money, many people have a very odd relationship with it. They may fear it, they may hoard it, they may spend it like water, they may be pennywise and pound-foolish, they may have wildly varied attitudes to risk. Quite commonly, they will be in denial, not wanting to talk about it, brushing it aside. Any of these attitudes are clearly unhelpful and contribute to the tragically high scrapheap of business failures.

It would be as well for governments to address this issue, and try to help relieve those worries, rather than leaving it to individuals to learn about money, as best they can, from parents who, in all probability, suffer from the same fears and thus pass them on, or schools, which are silent on the subject, and, almost certainly equally ignorant about it—and for much the same reasons. We are treated to all sorts of subjects at school which are vastly less important than 'Financial Understanding,' a subject title I have just made up, and don't think appears on any school curriculum.

Against such an unhelpful background, it is little wonder few aircraft receive the right fuel. Before you wade in blindly and begin making inevitable mistakes, consider—with great honesty—what your own relationship with money is and, where a little learning and insight might help you.

## The Eker Approach

There are many wise books out there to help us rethink our relationship with money. T Harv Eker, in his book *The Millionaire Mindset,* teaches a simple, but quite outstanding model, aimed at individuals, but which works effectively for business too. Essentially, he takes the lessons from George Clason's classic *The Richest Man in Babylon* and tells his readers to do this with their money:

1. Take turnover including VAT
2. Put the VAT in a VAT reserve account
3. Put a provision for tax in a tax reserve account
4. You now have an ex VAT, ex tax, pre cost figure
5. Put 50% of 4 into a necessities account (to cover all costs)
6. Put 10% of 4 into a long term savings to invest account
7. Put 10% of 4 into a savings to spend on short term projects account
8. Put 10% of 4 into an education account
9. Put 10% of 4 into a charity (or giving) account; and finally
10. Put the last 10% of 4 into a money for fun account—and blow it.

This is outstanding advice, because it deals with our two otherwise conflicting needs: to save and to spend. Harv's method allows for the fast building of net assets. A profit and loss account is all very well, but a strong balance sheet is even better. I highly recommend reading his book.

# A Note on Accountants

It would be easy to stop reading now and tell me 'Oh, my accountant handles all of that'. But the chances are, they don't. It's pretty likely you need to fire them and think again. You may think I am going too far, but I'm saying that as an entrepreneur who was originally an accountant. So, let me tell you why.

Traditional accountants, on the whole, do very little for their smaller clients; perhaps because those smaller clients do not generate a lot of income for them. They usually opt out of the vital initial bookkeeping. This is madness and it is also counter-productive. I'll go further. Those who do this are a disgrace to their profession.

Just a few years ago, one of the UKs' big five accounting firms spent a fortune on a campaign to attract such clients, on a grand scale, from smaller firms. Not long afterwards, they abandoned the scheme. To me, that speaks volumes.

Secondly, accountants often do another annoying thing. They don't warn their clients of the danger of not knowing where they are financially at all times. I have often heard the idea promoted that businesses need to be a certain size before they can justify paying for monthly management accounts. This is abject nonsense. Without a financial dashboard—the light that should guide every business—they may not get to the appropriate size, whatever that might be.

# Getting Accounting Right

There are of course some brilliant exceptions; accountants and firms who have modernised with the times and who get to the heart of what any person in business, big or small, needs. So here's what the ideal accountant looks like, for the modern entrepreneur...

- **THEY WILL BE DIGITAL**
  It is vital that all businesses set themselves up on a robust cloud-based accounting system from the beginning. Cloud-based accounting solutions remove any excuse not to be on top of the figures at all times, and unless you are very techy or a finance whizz, it is far better to have your accountant do this for you. Use xero for digital invoicing, hubdoc (which is part of xero) for receipts and expenses, all synced with your online banking. It's easy. Sometimes, if you have a smaller budget, you can take care of those processes yourself, then use your accountant to manage and evaluate the figures. Whether business owners want to take this essential step, or not, they will very shortly have to, when tax is made fully digital. Make sure you're prepared.

- **THEY WILL ALWAYS BE THERE FOR YOU**
  A good accountant should always be at the end of the phone. No charging per call. No obstacles

to getting information and advice. Pay a monthly retainer, expect unlimited support, and don't forget it's all online, so you can also check your figures yourself, any time, day or night.

- **THEY CAN MENTOR YOU ABOUT MONEY**
Your accountant should make things easy for you to understand. They should demystify accounting processes rather than acting like keepers at the gate. Don't be afraid of looking ignorant or uninformed—let them train you and help you understand. Working closely with a good accountant will improve your psychology about money no end.

- **THEY WILL GIVE YOU REGULAR AND USEFUL REPORTS**
They'll work with you to ensure that the headings in the chart of accounts, under which revenue and cost items are gathered, are set out in a way that is likely to produce meaningful management information.

Accounting should become a habit and be done daily. They will help you to produce monthly accounts—and set budgets to measure against the actual figures—detailing the percentage that each cost heading bears to total costs, so you can easily see the relevance of particular line items. 5–10% contingencies have their place in the original setting of budgets, but as we become more familiar with the regular monthly figures, they are often replaced, in practice, by known figures. Small numbers, added together, can amount to big, or even very big, numbers. To an extent that it can sometimes be hard to believe. This is why we need budgets, and to review the figures they throw up, at least once a month. Getting familiar with them. The old adage about counting the pennies is still as true as it ever was.

- **THEY WILL HELP YOU SEE THE FUTURE IN THE PRESENT**

To get to a reliable set of monthly management accounts takes at least three, sometimes as much as six, months, from the outset. Creating figures you can rely upon is a bit like weeding a garden—it comes from reviewing the figures monthly and polishing them. It takes work. But, after the first twelve months' figures, you will have the benefit of comparables from the same period in the previous year, so you become more familiar with seasonal patterns. The value of this simply cannot be overstressed. I recommend setting a management meeting, in the third week of every month, to review the figures to the end of the previous month. At each meeting, it is worth updating bank balances, and aged lists of debtors and creditors, to the date of the meeting, as it is important to have the latest figures for these when you meet.

- **THEY WILL ADVISE ON BUSINESS STRUCTURES**
  Your accountant should also provide you with advice about the relative advantages of trading as a sole proprietor, unlimited partnership, limited liability partnership (LLP) or limited company. At the time of writing, incorporating as a limited company probably offers the biggest advantages—with both the lowest tax rate and the protection of limited liability—but limited liability partnerships are also attractive, acting as a hybrid between sole tradership and unincorporated partnerships and the more formal structure of a limited company.

- **THEY WILL MAKE YOU DO WHAT YOU HAVE TO DO**
  The accountant's other contribution to the proceedings will be in assisting you with compliance matters: advising on choice of accounting date, filing limited company or LLP accounts with Companies House, providing confirmation statements for the same, and filing returns for Income and Corporation taxes, VAT, PAYE and NHI.

Once those systems are in place, and all other things being equal, your business' chances of survival and growth will increase exponentially. Armed with a robust accounting system, and a determination to keep it up to date, it is now down to you to use it in the same way as a careful driver uses the dashboard in the car. Here are some more specific things for you to think about...

# Defining Prices

Whether for goods or services, prices can be flexible, and business owners should remember this. There is often a tendency to think of prices as being the result of some percentage mark up on various costs, but it is better to consider them in the light of what customers might be willing to pay—in other words, their perceived value of the goods or services being provided—which is a very different thing. Covering all costs is very important, but it should not be how we determine prices. Remember that any price increase will filter directly through to the bottom line, with no additional costs attached to it. A robust attitude to periodic price increases is an essential ingredient in creating a profitable business.

# Profit's Sanity, Turnover's Vanity

You may have heard it said that 'Profit's Sanity and Turnover's Vanity': this is 100 per cent true. Turnover is, actually, of itself, entirely irrelevant. Making profits, retaining a part of them, and building a balance sheet is what business should be all about. Thus, the control of costs is at least as important as pricing. Bear in mind that every cost, in isolation, looks small, but add them together and you'll usually get a very nasty shock.

# Cash Is King

Of course, 'Cash is King' and if you run out of it, the party stops in a nanosecond, often in a very dramatic way. So, cashflow management is always of the most immediate importance. Always watch the level of funding in the business, the weekly or monthly burn rate, thereby ensuring, if the working capital fund is diminishing, and needs replenishing, that you start on such fund-raising at least six months before you run out. Ensuring that you have at least six months money, at all times, is vital—most small businesses only have working capital to last them for three months or less. The reason why six months' money is so important is simply this: if you don't have that buffer, you may not have time to replenish your coffers, except on unfavourable terms, before you run out. Negotiating with lenders or investors, when you are already in a hole, can put you at a serious disadvantage. And, it may kill your business.

Putting aside money monthly for income or company taxes, VAT and PAYE, along with other key reserves, is essential to avoid finding yourself unable to pay any of these when they fall due. Failure to do so will not help your reputation.

# Too Much Cash?

Having too much capital makes it more likely to be wasted (see attitudes to money above). Having too little has the effect of wasting too much management time trying to balance the books. Having about enough is a good place to be, since it avoids overspending—all too easy to do in an over generously funded start up. Hopefully, those providing the money will bring something extra to the party—by way of sector experience, contacts, business wisdom and so on, over and above their financial investment—and very often that something extra can be a lot more useful than money itself. Picking the right providers of money is hugely important. You need to make sure that your interests are aligned with theirs in terms of objectivity, returns and timescales. The sharing of ownership, where not fair, will backfire.

# Fixed Costs and Variable Costs

Knowing the split between your fixed costs, and variable costs, is also extremely important. Once your fixed costs are covered, the rest is profit, after allowing for the variable costs involved in each extra transaction—this is called Break Even Point, or Break Even, and is essential to include in your calculations.

## Chasing Debts and Training Debtors

When you review your budgets monthly, other than the financial result for the month, you need to keep a keen eye on your debtors, creditors and bank balances, which are key financial health performance indicators. They must be watched like a hawk. Debtors will look a lot better if you adopt a policy like Jeff Bezos did at Amazon—'you want to order a book on Amazon, it's cash down with order, or no book, I am afraid, Sir'.

If you are being paid too slowly, you will start to pay too slowly, and problems will thus build up on the road ahead. Your suppliers will start to be less keen to deal with you. If you want to be more gentle with debtor collection, set up automatic reminders on xero, and adopt a follow up-method, persistently, and politely, chasing debtors, using a mixture of email and phone calls—getting an agreed date for payments, and chasing up on that date. You will train them. Pretty soon they will start to comply, or it becomes embarrassing for them to have to keep taking your calls or fielding your chaser emails. Better still, use gocardless to set up what are effectively direct debits for you to pull in the cash.

If debtors become delinquent, just get rid of them, having collected as much of the debt as you think you can, if need be, with the aid of debt collectors. It's simple, if you have done the work, and they have not paid within your agreed timescales, then they have stolen your money—and none of us need that.

## Managing Losses

From time to time we all make losses. Losses, while painful, are usually more instructive than profits, and almost certain to happen, from time to time, especially in the early life of a business. This is the key reason why every start up needs to have an adequate amount of working capital from the outset. It is good to try to keep the outgoings pretty lean, in a new business, until it starts to become profitable. It takes time to build a customer base, and learn from many initial lessons, before the books start to balance.

## And Remember...

Don't be scared of taking on costs. For businesses to grow this is essential. Costs are fine, so long as they are covered by equal or greater revenues. It is the return on the investment of money which is critical, not the cost itself seen in isolation. But bear in mind that you can make profits by BOTH increasing sales AND controlling costs. And, you must do both.

And finally, be careful not to be over reliant on one or more large customers. If you lose them, or they hold you to ransom by paying you too slowly, it can kill your business. At the beginning this may be inevitable, but it is something to watch and move away from as soon as possible.

There is a huge amount to think about, when you are trying to steer a young company through the shark infested waters of the business world, but maintaining a very tight grip on the finances is beyond vitally important, and greatly reduces your chances of failure. Keep that aircraft fuelled. At all times. No exceptions.

# CHAPTER SIX

# ASSEMBLING YOUR FLIGHT CREW

Your business. You lead it. You're the key entrepreneur. The buck stops with you. If you want to make your business great, it's up to you. No one else. Scary thought, maybe. You've got to recruit, get the key people in place, build your team, set and chair your meetings. And multi task.

You need customers, suppliers, advisors, investors, lenders, full time employees and freelancers to want to work with, or in, your business. So, the job starts with you. You have got to stand out. Be authentic. Always go the extra mile. Walk the walk, not just talk the talk. If you want your team to become the best they can be—strong and united—you must always lead—and lead by example.

But you can't do everything. You must make sure you have the right skills on board. You will need a multi skilled, and diverse, team.

When you start a business, the first, and most crucial, decision you will make is who to start it with. Choosing a co-founder is like getting married. And, founder conflict can be just as ugly as divorce. Optimism abounds at the start of every relationship. It is unromantic to think soberly about what could go wrong. So, people don't. But, please fix firmly in your mind, if you haven't learnt it already from painful experience, that if co-founders develop irreconcilable differences, the business becomes the victim. Founders should, ideally, have a pre-history together, before they start a business. Otherwise, they are just rolling the dice.

In Chapter One, we looked at what it takes to get an entrepreneurial business off the ground—balancing the conflicting skill sets of the Technician, the Manager and the Entrepreneur so they are effective. It starts with a skills audit—are you Technician, Manager, Entrepreneur all in one (i.e. a sole tradership) or are you bringing in others? If the latter, work out which of you will fill each of those roles, and then go on to audit how strong each of you is in all of the areas below:

- People/team building
- Marketing
- Selling
- Negotiation
- Finance
- Administration
- Strategy (conception)
- Operations (execution)
- Tech/ systems

and then find out each person's:

- Attitude to risk, and
- Whether they see themselves as a brake or an accelerator.

From the results of the above audit, you will need to decide, from the beginning, who does what, allowing everyone to play to their strengths. Make sure you really spend time on this—getting to know yourself, and the others, right from the get go. And, remember to only work with a group of people who you like and trust, and who like and trust each other. Otherwise, it's misery.

# Being A Leader

You're number one on the team. You have got to be inspiring in order to ensure that others are inspired. You have got to demonstrate patience—as well as impatience—on occasions. You've got to be decisive. Firm in decision, while being considerate in execution. You've got to listen—and be prepared to hear what you perhaps don't want to hear.

You've got to build your team around you. It goes without saying that you have got to know at all times where you are going to lead them. And, if conditions change and you need to change direction, make sure you keep them briefed, and hold their attention, while you do.

Think of your team as an orchestra. You are the conductor. You choose the music, the players, the instruments. You have got to build that team so well that you can get a symphony out of them. Every time. This is how seriously you must approach team building, as well as anticipating the huge joy of a bravura performance.

You must be able to manage, delegate, and supervise. This last—supervision—is most important. Mere delegation, followed by the assumption that all will be well, usually doesn't work. That's merely delegation by abstention. Delegate in that way, and disaster awaits you.

You must nurture your team and watch them grow. Be caring and compassionate. Praise them in public, and, if you must reprimand them, do it in private.

You should try to nurture an open style, being open, being human, even showing your vulnerability at times. Vulnerability can greatly increase credibility. None of us like people who seem cold and inhuman.

A human approach to running your team will be far more effective than a rules-based culture. Allowing your team to have fun—and, sometimes, having fun with them—will help make sure they are there for you when times are tough.

Never, ever, be afraid to ask a question, even if it may sound stupid, or you might fear showing your ignorance. There is no such thing as a stupid question.

Having the welfare of your team members in the

forefront of your mind will pay rich dividends—especially when they are, themselves, going through hard times. Make sure that they feel valued, respected, cared for and appreciated. Do as you would be done by.

Remember, above all, that people take most decisions for emotional reasons. They may justify them with logic, but the underlying reason for almost every decision is, at root, an emotional one.

# Hiring...

You come to recruit a new person or new people. Perhaps you haven't recruited before. And so, maybe, you fall into the trap of hiring the wrong person (through lack of understanding of what work they are going to do, or perhaps by interviewing them badly). You hire them fast. And then you waste hours and hours agonising, forever, before you fire them.

It should be the other way around—you should hire slowly, and fire quickly. Take time creating the job, skills and personality specifications. Interview at least twice, maybe three times. Interview in the company of a colleague. Compare notes afterwards.

Only hire when you are sure. A note of caution—you may have put out an advertisement, got replies in double figures, done a lot of interviewing, shortlisted, and still found you are underwhelmed with either, or both, the short list or final potential choice. In these circumstances, do NOT hire.

Most interviews are stilted affairs, where the candidate is on best behaviour, and the employer asks the wrong questions, or insufficiently penetrating questions. I want to know a lot more about the person I am hiring. I want to know lots of things that are maybe not on the candidate's CV. Here are some examples.

Is he or she:
- A completer finisher?
  Or someone who leaves loose ends?
- A clock watcher?
  Or someone who will stay until the job's done?
- A workaholic? Balanced between work and play? Or Lazy?
- Someone who takes pressure well?
  Or becomes stressed and cracks?
- A self starter?
  Or someone who needs daily spoon feeding?
- Committed? Or looking over their shoulders for the next opportunity?
- A multi tasker? Or someone who can only take on one thing at a time?
- Motivated?
- Personally well organised?
- Self disciplined?
- Punctual? A good time keeper?

- Capable of scheduling and managing their timetable?
- Capable of coming up with coherent strategies?
- Reliable?
- Honest?
- Trustworthy?
- Someone who demonstrates integrity?
- Responsible?
- In possession of good values?
- An empire builder who likes to take credit? Or someone who shares it?
- A team player? Or a lone wolf?
- Prepared to share weaknesses?
- Willing to tell you about past successes, as well as failures and disappointments?
- Well presented? Aware of their appearance?
- A communicator? Or someone who plays their cards close to their chests?
- Someone who helps others? Or demonstrates selfishness?
- Aware of where they want to be in two to three years' time?
- Likeable?
- From a secure and happy background?
- In a happy relationship?
- Interested, spending their spare time, in outside sports, hobbies, or passions, or one track minded?
- Interesting? This is so important.

(Beware of those who are not).
- A reader? If so, what do they read? Ask them.

So, there you go. Lots and lots of questions. Probably better spread over two or three interviews, fed in, gently, and not fired off staccato—hopefully by more than one person—not least to enable the comparing of notes, allow time for reflection, and perhaps revert to probing deeper on the next occasion. Work out, between you, who is the best judge of character. Defer to them.

Build in some silences too, giving them time to talk or ask you questions.

I am a great believer in adding in both skills tests, at interview, as well as posing 'what if' questions to see how candidates might deal with typical challenging issues they are likely to encounter in the course of their work.

I am always amazed by how very few of the types of questions, which I have listed above, are put to candidates. Equally, it astonishes me how often employees leave, probably unhappily, after quite a short time in their new position, as a result of the interviewer's failure to build proper foundations at the interview stage. A failure caused by misunderstandings arising from those poor roots. Perhaps, dare I say it, from a lack of respect for the new recruit.

# … And Firing

Always give your new recruit a trial period, and, if things are not working well during that trial period, end the trial, straight away, and let them go. If, for whatever reason, at ANY time, you discover that you have got a hire wrong, admit it, cut your losses, and bring it to an end, as quickly as possible, for everyone's sake.

I have found that, in organisations with less than about 30 employees, there isn't the emotional capacity to carry any passengers who are unhelpful, moody, selfish, or unable to play their part in a team. If you find that you have taken on one of these, reverse the mistake quickly, and remember to learn from that mistake and take more care with the next hiring.

For those who make it into the organisation, and who you decide to keep, make sure you get them to write down, within their first three months, what they see in your company which they think is good, that which is less so, and what changes they think should be made. Finally, what part they might like to play in bringing about such changes.

This will send them a message, early on, that you are listening to them, and value their views. After three months they will have become part of the furniture, and will probably have lost their fresh incomer's view—which, when shared, can help an organisation so much. So, get in there early.

# Creating A Positive Work Culture

Hires in place, it is time to build your team. While there must be ground rules, hopefully you will grow an organisation where people can breathe freely and make contributions which will be valued. Let them know who got a result, who scored a goal—and tell everyone. Praise success—and share it around.

Develop a climate of support. Encourage individuals. Bring them in. Get them excited—people can usually find more energy for things when they are excited. Keep them happy. If they're not, find out why, and do something about it.

Review every member of the team at least twice a year—take plenty of time over it—help them to set goals for their performance, and support them to achieve those goals. Take trouble to get to know each one as a person.

Decide whether their last year was good, satisfactory or bad. Help them to feel supported as part of the team. Find out what they found difficult or stressful. Ask them what they found most rewarding. Work out, with them, their priorities for the coming year. Find out how they can see themselves improving their contribution to the company—and the team. Get clear on what training could support them. And so on. And make sure all of this is written down.

At least once a year, take your whole team out for a day to do something fun. Bond with them. Not only will everyone enjoy this, but it will add a broader dimension to relationships within the team, and help them to support each other more—as fellow human beings, not just as work colleagues. Once each of them knows more about the personal lives of each other, they will relate to them far better, and want to support and help them more.

And then there's meetings. But, not too many. They all must have a purpose. A monthly management meeting is the staple—the agenda broadly needs to cover:

- Apologies for absence
- Minutes of the last meeting
- Blue sky thinking—(we need this early in the meeting or we will be tired, and ready to get away, when we get to it—traditionally at the end of the meeting)
- Issues arising
- Finance
- Business development
- Marketing
- The team
- Any other business (which should be pre announced), and
- Date of the next meeting.

You must chair these meetings. Make sure you allow enough time for contributions from all those attending. But, you must also watch the clock like a hawk. Tell everyone in advance what time you intend the meeting to finish. Perhaps also brief them on how much time to allow for each agenda item. Move things on as needed to keep matters progressing on track. Most meetings are chaired horribly badly—practise so you keep your team interested, and keen to attend the next one. Your key people must attend. Papers should go out at least two days ahead of the meeting, and be taken as read once the meeting starts.

It is critical to decide what you want to get out of the meeting. Have a whiteboard in the meeting, should there be a need to develop ideas during the blue sky thinking session—take a photo of the board with your phone and type the notes up to go out with the minutes. We spoke at the beginning of the book about the new world of Zoom. Did you know that it had a 'Whiteboard' function under the option to 'Share Screen'?' Wonderful for this. And if you get everyone to share their ideas in the 'Chat' box, you can save that feed to your computer. Easy and efficient.

You can also record a session on Zoom (as long as you have everyone's permission). If not, then at the very least, someone should take detailed notes, during each meeting, in preparation for creating the minutes. This is hugely important. It is not about bureaucracy. It is about ensuring that, after each meeting, everyone can be completely clear on exactly what was agreed in the meeting. Sometimes minutes can waffle. They must not. They must be able to answer this question: 'What did we decide to do?'

The minutes should go out, within two days of the meeting at most, while events are still fresh in everybody's minds. After each management meeting, review the proceedings—what went well, what not so well. And learn from it.

Fix the meeting dates for every month at the beginning of each year. Make sure they are in everyone's diaries. Treat them as sacrosanct. There is ever the temptation to cancel team meetings, because they don't seem urgent and important. Resist it. They are a vital pillar supporting how the business works.

There will be some subjects which require a meeting on their own—with a single-issue agenda. These will usually be for important projects which take time to develop. Often these will be longer meetings. Don't try to squeeze them in to management meetings, where it will be impossible to do proper justice to them. This simply results in the key participators feeling frustrated and demotivated.

Give projects inspiring names—this will add to the motivation to make a success of them. Discussions for a fund raising will seem rather more glamorous if the subcommittee responsible is working on 'Broadsword' rather than 'that refinancing idea'.

Make sure you have a suitable, quiet, room, with a decent sized table and comfortable chairs, in which to conduct these meetings. If this is impossible where you work, it may be worth taking a room locally to ensure you can provide this kind of environment. If you cannot, your meetings will be a lot less effective. I have had to remind many of my clients, in the past, about this most basic requirement.

And, finally, no external interruptions during the meeting. Few phone calls cannot wait for an hour. They'd have to if you were in someone else's important meeting, so there is no excuse for letting them into your own.

Before we leave this point, you might, at the current time especially, be attending a a meeting by zoom link. You might not be used to the technology. So, here are a few tips: Be on time, dress appropriately, find a professional looking background, sit in the centre of your screen—make sure it is high enough and your face is lit. You don't get a second chance to make a first impression.

## Outsourcing

In addition to your in-house staff, you should outsource services that you need less frequently than every day. Examples will be accountancy and compliance, IT, legal matters and so on. You may also need other skilled professionals, on a less frequent basis, such as those who are part of my Runway Advisors collective.

You need a really good accountant, just as you need a really good person, or persons, to keep you up to speed on the tech road.

Lawyers you need less. Someone said you only need them to buy a house, divorce your wife, make a will or sue somebody. But actually, in corporate life, even in small corporate life, they are a lot more useful than that, and you do need a good general counsel close enough to you so you can call him or her on an as and when basis. Legal matters that might be on your agenda would include, in no particular order:

- Company formation
- Articles of Association
- Setting up your registered office
- Company secretarial matters
- Confirmation statements
- Changes of directors
- Directors service agreements
- Directors loan accounts
- Shareholder agreements
- Share certification
- Sale and purchase agreements
- Terms of business
- Privacy clauses, and
- Other ad hoc matters

Your accountant might handle some of these, but, for matters like shareholder agreements, which can have a massive impact on the business—and its owners—if things go wrong, only a good lawyer will do.

Make sure, with all of your outside advisors, that you like and trust each of them, and that they are both competent and affordable.

## Words of Wisdom

I want to end this chapter with a mixed bag of tips for the entrepreneurial leader who is managing people—a team (both on the books, or working on an advisory basis), customers, suppliers, lenders and all the others who form part, in some way, of the daily life of the business:

- Only ever work with people where there is mutual respect and mutual impact.
- Remember that life is not always black and white—there are shades of grey. Have your rules of engagement, but also be able to be flexible. The exception proves the rule.
- People talk about hard skills, and then mention soft skills as a bolt on. Soft skills are the more important.
- Leadership involves, or should involve, doing nothing for quite a lot of the time.
- Keeping your door ajar to people is a better rule

than keeping it fully open at all times.

- Keep suppliers on their toes—make them aware that your team are always making comparisons with their competitors on price, quality and service provided.
- On a well-run board of directors, you need someone who is a brake, to balance someone who is an accelerator, and an operations person should be counterbalanced by a strategic person.
- Remember that there is a world of difference between leading and managing.
- Keep a daily log of the achievements of both your business and the individuals working in it—share these with your team. When things are difficult, referring back to them will give you, and them, a massive shot in the arm, and keep you going. It is so easy to forget—in the cut and thrust of the business day—just how far we have come.
- Get clear that, in most business situations, there are three elements—the task, the team, and each individual involved. For a successful outcome, all three parts need managing.
- Try to be kind and forgiving. Practise it to get better. People (sometimes including yourself!) will test your patience. So, practise forgiving yourself, and others. Life is short and time is precious.
- Lastly, remember above all else to work only for, and with, those you respect—or, yes, even love.

# CHAPTER SEVEN

# THE AIR BENEATH YOUR WINGS

This is happening. You are doing alright. Foundations in place, people assembled, clear vision planned out, finances working well. But you could have the best product, and the best business systems, and still fail. Why? Because you don't have enough air under your wings to lift you higher. This thrust, this uplift, comes from the marketing you do to make your business soar.

A study of past episodes of the programme *Dragons Den* can be very helpful, if only to underpin how essential it is to truly understand your market. Marketing can—wrongly—be seen as the soft side of business, the after-thought. It's always astonishing to me how little companies think about, or invest in, good marcomms. How even those that do have things in place rarely have a strategy underpinning it all. How reluctant start-ups can be to pay for expert services to make them fly. The general attitude: *We can write some copy, can't we? We can take a few pictures! We can make a promo film! Social media?*

*It's easy isn't it? And the website's alright, I just knocked it up on Squarespace.*

No. Wrong. You might do enough to hover off the ground, but you will never reach steady flight. Many see marketing as the first cost to go when the winds blow. Such an unwise decision will usually be the first stage in the death of the business. Whatever happens in the business, no matter how bad things get, NEVER, EVER compromise on your brand, or stop actively marketing your products or services.

It's more than a snappy slogan, a pretty website or an active Twitter account. Everything starts with amassing a detailed knowledge of your competition and the size of the market. And establishing if there actually is a gap in the market for your offering, and indeed whether there is a workable market in that gap. Is it a narrow but deep niche? Or is it bigger than that? Where does your offering fit into it? What is your Unique Selling Proposition? Is it unique enough? Or does it need tweaking to become so? Once those facts are established, we need to get focussed on how we are going to penetrate the market successfully.

# Facing In / Facing Out

Speak to any good marketing expert, and they will divide your thinking into internal and external. Facing in, and facing out. Facing in can be thought of as getting the inside of the shop ready. Facing out is the shop window. It is so common in business to do the latter without the former.

- **FACING IN.** This is essentially the production of a marcomms strategy, a clear one-sentence USP, strong branding and collateral, a clear website driven by easy UX (user experience), engaging copy and great design, SEO set up in the back-end of the website, consistent and engaging social media channels, measurement in place for all your social media and website traffic, Mailchimp (or similar) set up, definitive messaging, an identified audience, a list of people both online and offline to engage with, and an achievable timeline of what rolls out and when.

- **FACING OUT.** The window dressing to entice customers in. We're often quick to work on the latter. But how often when people create a beautiful shop window, do you go inside to find piles of hotchpotch goods and unclear aisles, and no one at the till to take your cash? Facing out covers Website content, social media posts and engagement, email marketing, PR (online and offline), events, campaigns, advertising, networking, collaborations and partnerships.

In short, facing in is what stories you will tell, to whom, when, why, and how. Facing out is putting all those stories out into the world, monitoring their success, and adapting them along the way.

As I said, it's more than a slogan and a website. It is the very core understanding of your business, and how you communicate that understanding to others, both inside your business and outside to an audience. It's how you make money. How you build a brand. How you achieve your vision. It's the air to make you fly.

## Defining Your Business

Let's start at the beginning. Do you actually know what your business is? That might sound ridiculous. But when you begin writing this down, you'll see how tough a one-sentence summary is. But you need it. Right now.

Start with rambling. Put down everything your business is. Not just what you do or what you offer, or how much things cost. But what your overall ethos is. What world you want to create. What stories you want to tell. Don't dismiss this as whimsical nonsense. You'll only get those customers if you can communicate heart to heart.

Now edit this down to a page. Use headings if you like. Lots of businesses find it useful to have a bullet point mission statement of sorts. Start sentences with 'We believe' and see what comes out.

Now turn this into one paragraph.

Now reduce it down to a single sentence. Read it out to a few people. Does it achieve what you want it to achieve? Get their feedback, and keep polishing it.

Do you understand it? Truly understand it? Have you internalised it so that it becomes second nature to you? If not, no one else will get it. Are you filled with passion about it? If not, why not? And, if you are not, you might find it hard to fire up others with it. Make sure you love your business, love your offering. Ensure that it stands out.

You are going to do a lot with this summary you create. It will become your 'About Us' on your website. It will become the 'Business Overview' on planning or finance documents. It will become the 'Elevator Pitch' we have already discussed.

And that one sentence will work harder for you than you think. It will be the one sentence in your social media bios. It will be the subhead beneath your company name. It might become your slogan, or hero sentence on your website front page. It will be the way you make sure everyone who works for you is on the same page. And in time, it will become the sentence people quote to each other, when they're telling people about you.

# Developing Your Messaging

Remember what I said before—from the heart, to the heart. You have to make the shift from thinking of your company as something that DOES something, to something that IS something. A brand. An ethos. A feeling. Yes, I did say a feeling. Whether you're selling sofas or services, emotion MUST run through how you present them. Focus on the benefits of the product or service and the problems that it solves. Sell the 'sizzle not the steak'. Buyers are only interested in receiving relief for their specific problems or delivery of their desires. Features and figures are of no interest to them. Watch any car or cosmetic ad to see exactly what I mean.

Consider what your audience needs. Consider their problems, their vulnerabilities. Consider what it is that they actually want you to solve for them. They don't want a new sofa. They want to feel proud of their home. They want to be able to enjoy time relaxing with all their family.

Identifying need is rooted in the concept of 'The 8 Rs'. The eight things that buyers need to be satisfied for them:

- RECOGNITION
- REJUVENATION
- RELAXATION
- RELIEF

- RELIGION
- REMUNERATION
- REVENGE
- ROMANCE

Well, on second thoughts, maybe forget revenge, but what about the other seven? If you can help people to scratch those itches, you will be well on your way to profitability.

This is great for your initial engagement. Hook them up, heart to heart, and they're more likely to want to find out more. This is where features and figures and smallprint comes in. That's when they decide whether to buy. But meet their emotional needs first—make them feel like you know them—and they're more likely to convert. And beyond that, more likely to stay.

Because your messaging isn't just about getting people into your shop. It's about making them feel so good they come back again and again. That's where marketing comes into its own. All flights need a constant supply of fresh air under those wings. Make them like you and trust you. Complete a sale. Capture their data and needs. Keep in touch with them. Let the relationship evolve.

Remember that people buy people. They've got to like you, trust you, feel you are competent, and, finally, be happy with your prices or fees. That's all. People do things—buy things—for emotional reasons (regardless of how they might justify their buying decisions with logic). So, what comes from the heart goes to the heart. Every time. Take trouble with would-be customers, at times when they are not buying—bringing them closer to the point of purchase—thereby preparing for the time when they will be ready to buy.

You can expect it to take about six or seven interactions before someone trusts you enough to buy or sign up. Interactions might be adverts, social media activity, word of mouth, product visibility, articles, or direct emails from you. Through these interactions, they build up a sense of your '6 U's':

- URGENT
- UNIQUE
- USEFUL
- ULTRA SPECIFIC
- USER FRIENDLY, and
- UNQUESTIONABLY PROVED

## Your Marketing Strategy

So, how do we create a pipeline of prospects, and how do we get them in the mood to buy our offerings? We need to consider a variety of continuums and decide where our activities will sit. They are:

1. **Huge mass market / Small niche targeted audience**

   Whether we are going out to very large numbers of people, a tiny percentage of which are likely to buy from us, or whether we want to go out to a much smaller, already qualified, market, from whom we might expect to get a much higher take up rate. The difference between broadcasting—and what the late Sir Terry Wogan called 'Narrow casting'—is achieved through the creation of a more individual and personal communication.

2. **Active marketing (outreach) / Passive marketing (inbound)**

   A passive strategy suggests that we establish ourselves as an authority in a certain area, providing very valuable information, without charge, to our audience, and looking to them to find our company. Smart SEO techniques can be part of this too. Or whether we adopt a more active outreach strategy of communicating with our targets regularly. Outreach marketing is about repeat emails, repeat points of contact, lots of fresh content, PR, appearances, advertising. In short, more budget, more people, more resources.

   Inbound passive marketing is always cooler than touting. Think about how you can 'be of service'. Offer things for free to download on your site. Offer talks and events to bring people to you. I have advised several service-based clients to run monthly breakfasts for key targets and influencers—about a dozen guests at a time—getting one to give an address. This builds goodwill relatively cheaply over a delicious breakfast, and creates rapport. I have found this works very effectively. No hard sale needed.

3. **ALL ONLINE / ALL OFFLINE**
Some businesses naturally tend to one side or the other. Ideally they combine the two. But when you are making this decision, remember you are serving the business, not yourself. You might not like social media, but perhaps your business absolutely needs it. And if you get the right person in charge of it, you can see the impact without doing it yourself.

4. **SHORT TERM GAIN / LONG TERM LOYALTY**
Again, different strokes for different folks. Maybe you want to shift a lot of tickets for a one-off festival. Maybe you offer an expensive, luxury product that can also be a repeat buy for a devoted kind of customer. Think about what pay-offs you need, and balance cashflow with sustainability.

5. **ORGANIC / STRATEGIC**
Is our approach to different groups of would-be customers going to be strategic, or more organic?

Whichever way, we need to get lots of fishing lines out on the river bank to attract those customers. The vast majority of businesses will need something around the middle of these spectrums. Your strategy will identify the pivot point. The pivot point might change as the reality of your business changes.

## Attracting Customers/Clients

Ultimately, it's a percentage game. I often suggest to clients that they approach five potential customers daily—they might use the telephone, email, letters or a mixture of all of the above. The key thing is to keep approaching five a day. Counting working days only, that's 1,300 prospects in a year. And will produce plenty of business. IF you do it EVERY SINGLE day.

Prospecting is an art. A good customer relationship management system will make this a lot easier. I use Hubspot which is cloud based, cheap, simple and effective. A good prospecting system will involve a process of recording and following up approaches. If it isn't easy and simple, it probably won't be done. It all starts with a good database which is regularly cleaned.

The most effective marketing campaigns will be a mixture of both online and offline. Using both to seek out innovative ways of getting new customers without leaving money on the table.

While, at the present time, the world thinks mainly online, offline can be extremely effective—involving communications by postcard (short), personal letter (longer) or telephone. The power of the short, handwritten, postcard, and longer, carefully crafted, personal letter cannot be overstated in this electronic age. Sending letters, marked 'Private & Confidential', by Special Delivery, can pack even more of a punch. It makes you stand out from the crowd who are not doing it. It gets you noticed.

## The Conveyor Belt

Whatever you do, it must be systematic and, as far as possible, automated. A little bit of time on marketing, when done well, can go a long way. Spend 40 minutes on a blog post, then upcycle that into social media posts, a newsletter, press articles, a talk, a downloadable document. We need a system to do all of this. One that is relentless. One that is easy to understand, and able to roll out offerings regularly to our audience. In essence, 'a conveyor belt'. A marketing and communications programme, designed especially for us. One that can be rolled out daily, weekly, monthly, quarterly, bi annually and annually, with minimum head scratching. This conveyor belt will deal with:

- BULLETINS (sometimes called newsletters, but not by me, as that makes them sound very boring!). Perhaps monthly, which contain news and editorial, flowing in an order—like your daily paper—that customers, and would be customers, can get familiar with.

- EMAILS, with clever, eye catching, subject titles—image rich, sometimes with videos, never boring—using headlines and subtitles to keep the reader reading—and with calls to action, and links throughout the email. Don't worry when people unsubscribe. Unsubscribing helps to clean your list.

- SOCIAL MEDIA is your shop window. Consider instagram (my favourite), linkedIn (another favourite), twitter and facebook. All of these have different purposes. All are useful. But remember to treat them like separate TV channels with different audiences, needing different approaches. LinkedIn Automated Lead Generation can be outstandingly effective and provides a very quick return on investment—and takes up very little time.

- AUTORESPONDER, to communicate regularly with subscribers. I use MailerLite for this.

- BLOGS, ARTICLES, EDITORIAL CONTENT, on your website—a lot of which can be written well ahead of time to ensure that they can be posted regularly to avoid the usual long gaps in most corporate blogging programmes. Don't forget that you can repurpose earlier material. Always keep in mind that your website is your shop. It is there to provide information. Also to showcase you, credentialise you, and, thus, build trust.

## Mix It Up

A complete marketing strategy will involve online, offline, social media, PR, production and copywriting. And remember one more thing: long copy still works, but keep it interesting. You need to hold your audience's attention, starting from the main headline, through sub headings, flicking through your text like skimming stones, right to the end. And they will do this so long as you don't bore them. Bore them, even with short copy, and you're dead.

Showcase your offerings in the clearest way. Remember not to always try to sell them. Instead, Show things. Make friends with people. Then they'll buy. Remember to keep in touch, and to follow up. It is easier to sell to an existing customer than to go out and find a new one. Creating a healthy pipeline is the best way to ensure that you always have a choice of which prospective customer you are going to take on. And keep testing—test, test, test.

Test small—and, only when it is working—roll out big.

One more thing. Don't forget to keep looking around and checking at all times. If, you don't see any sales people, you're the sales person.

# CHAPTER EIGHT

# THE PLANE THAT FLIES ITSELF

## 'LOOK, NO HANDS!'

Systems, systems, systems. Organised processes working together. Automated functions. An engine at the centre of them, making all the parts work synergetically. Pilot there to check and fine tune them. When you're flying well, in a top machine, it's often said it's like the plane 'just flies itself'.

The same is true of your business. And, yet, just how often do we find that those finely balanced systems aren't in place? Disorganised, chaotic, uncoordinated—that is why most businesses fail. You must harness systems to help you. Essentially, we must use every tool in the box to leverage ourselves away from wasting time on repetitive menial tasks. There is no need not to. Just create a great system, or a set of systems that work. And, then, YOU won't have to.

Some of our systems will be semi-manual—the guiding rule for all of them must be that they are unbureaucratic, simple to use and capable of saving us time, while keeping us focused.

New cloud-based systems and apps appear on a daily basis, to take away the stress and strain from one or other repetitive function, and provide ways—which have only been available for the last ten years or so—to help us substantially leverage repetitive tasks which previously took up hours and hours of our precious time. Accountancy is a good example.

Being on top of the admin is essential, because, when we're not, it becomes a thief of our time. And, into the bargain, it kills our fun.

This is really just part of getting the organisation and its routines under control—whether it's the filing system or something more sophisticated than that.

Systems only work when we have installed them extremely carefully and tested them properly. Sometimes they will need a little recalibration. Once we have taken the time and trouble to set them up, they can only give us greater freedom. Systems that work so we don't have to pull everything together with band aids and rubber bands.

When putting in systems, even if they are simple ones, it is best to create an overall plan first, and then get buy in to it. The more that a system can be adopted by all, or most of the members, of a team, the more effective it is likely to be—when communication can also be leveraged. And we only get buy in from the rest of the team, once they have understood the objective and persuasive reasons have been made to support it.

# Measurement

We also need to give some thought as to how we measure success—what we want to deliver, and by when, to what standard, with what key performance indicators built in, so that we can measure whether we have succeeded or fallen short of the mark.

It is tempting to merely download an app and start using it straight away, but joined up thinking pays dividends here. Having the patience, and taking the time, to develop systems which can be integrated with each other, is time well spent. We want our systems to be effective and to save time, not simply create work. The devil is ever present in the detail. Systems that half work are worse than none at all. This requires rigorous discipline, creating the right architecture for a system from the outset, and not putting up with half cooked solutions—staying on the case of whoever is responsible for delivering a fully functioning system that works consistently as it should. There is a wealth of really competent people out there who can make these things happen, at very affordable prices. Work hubs, across the country, act as a breeding ground for this massively important source of talent.

# Integrating Your Systems

Ideally, your business should have a simple map of the systems that it uses, and how they interact and integrate with each other. Systems that work, so that you don't have to work quite so hard, and what work you do can be on more amusing and productive things.

The best example of this is McDonalds, whose systems work well enough to enable each franchise to employ teenagers who you might otherwise have difficulty in persuading to tidy their rooms or make their beds.

Many, off the shelf, cloud-based systems have APIs (application programming interfaces) that enable them to be effortlessly integrated into other cloud-based systems. If it is possible to do this with your systems to avoid having to spend time and money on non-standard integrations, it is highly recommended, but sometimes we have to build bridges to link up some of the parts.

I use many cloud-based systems to help both my clients and myself—they have become so readily available, that we barely realise how many are already working for us. I use Hubspot and CamCard for contact management, MileIQ for recording mileage, HoursForTeams to record time, Trello to manage it, Doodle to fix meetings, Xero and Hubdoc for accounting, MailerLite and Flashissue for email communications, Apple Notes for planning, GoogleDocs for sharing documents. That's twelve for starters, and the list goes on.

We can only manage what we can measure, and so we need systems to do this for us in a timely way—not just on the financial front, but to gather all other important metrics and facts so as to enable us to take timely and well-informed decisions. And not just decisions, but also to enable us to implement things when they need implementing.

Some things still need to be offline—occasionally notes for clients, meetings—agendas and minutes.

## Make It Routine

Alongside this, we still need to focus on our own, and our team's, time management, in the old-fashioned way. I am a huge believer in routine. Getting into regular ways of doing things until they become habits. Two-to three-hour sessions, at most, timetabled for morning and afternoon. With breaks in between.

I batch process emails at certain times in the day. I use apple notes for reminders on a whole range of subjects. I allocate certain types of work to certain days. And I keep refining my processes. They work for me. Others will have different systems that work for them.

There will be times when the more techy among us should reverse mentor those, who are less techy, in technical matters. The less techy can then help the techies in areas where they are less strong. This is largely an age thing, and it should not be forgotten that experience can be very effectively traded for tech and vice versa. And it should be. It does not happen enough.

# CHAPTER NINE

# REFUELLING

You have everything in place. Your aircraft is off the ground. Enough air beneath your wings, enough fuel in the tank, a high-functioning engine, great pilot, great crew. You feel like you can keep flying forever. But of course you can't.

All businesses, like all aircraft, need to refuel. They need a service from time to time. They need modifications for changing conditions—changing weather, changing customers. As Bob Dylan put it, 'when you're not busy being born, you're busy dying'.

We network for a variety of reasons. We need to know the best ways to do it. We need to know how to negotiate with some of the people who we have networked with.

That all seems a bit nebulous. How do we dive in and start?

I am not going to try to set out here the technical processes of networking (save for one particular communication technique I sometimes use with cold contacts) because there are already plenty of books on the subject, written by those who specialise in networking, and who have turned it into an art form. I am writing this chapter principally on the subject of why we must become efficient networkers (and negotiators).

For the purposes of this book, I only want to share the *reasons* for networking. These are generally in order to:

1.  Recruit team members
2.  Find new clients
3.  Collaborate with others
4.  Find professional and commercial advisors
5.  Buy or sell a business... and so on.

From the outset it is also pretty important to identify the 'tribe' or tribes that you want to work with.

Networking, to me, is like beachcombing. Perhaps you have experienced walking the length of a long beach, looking at shells, pebbles, flotsam and jetsam, weathered pieces of wood, small fish, crustaceans and so on. Much of it is repetitive, unexciting, but then—something catches your eye. It might be a special shell, an unusual pebble, perhaps a piece of driftwood. I feel, in many ways, it is the same with people. When we start to see networking as a world of opportunity, where there are all sorts of intriguing people out there who we can help, and who can help us, then new vistas open. It brings the chance to add someone new to the little black book, with all the excitement that that entails. As I write this, I recall that I have met two new wonderful new people, in this way, in just the last week. And, the more we beachcomb for people, the better we do it.

And then we need to nurture those people and keep in touch. We need to stay focussed on how we can help them, just as much, if not more than, how they can help us. We need to be willing to invest time to find out how they tick and what they are looking for. We should be careful not to judge people, because opportunities so often come out of left field from the least expected sources. Listen to people, then sit back and watch.

As with doing good turns, helping somebody somewhere down the line, without asking for anything in return, can so often produce outstanding results sometime later, from a completely different source. It makes the world go around better, and being in it more fun. What comes around nearly always goes around too.

## Introduce Yourself

When I started out in the working world, over forty years ago, a lot of people obsessed about the need to be introduced. Some, amazingly to my mind, still do. This causes a lot of problems. While having doors opened for you by a heavy hitter could, on the face of it, bring advantages, more often than not, those advantages came with strings attached—potentially unrealistic expectations of your performance by the person to whom you are being introduced, and mis-selling of your offering by the introducer, being just two of these. That process could bring axe grinding opportunities for both the introducer and the contact he or she introduced you to. I cannot remember a single occasion where that method was effective.

To me, much more interesting, is self-introducing. The great advantage of this process is that it avoids any hidden agendas. It means that your offering, or reason for making contact, needs to be much better honed and much more precise.

Once you have decided to mainly use the unintroduced route, you will need to get braver, which is always a good thing. You will begin to recognise, more and more, the power of your little black book, and how vital it is to build it. I find it much more powerful than trying to get things airborne on the back of an introduction, and the expectation which that brings with it. Others may have different experiences, but that has been mine.

I'm going to share with you, now, one process that has always been foolproof for me. Remember, as you read this, the previous chapter with its emphasis on systems. Introductions are no different. And here's how it goes…

# The Write-Call-Meet Approach

Remember what we said about six or seven interactions to hook customers in? The same is true of networking and new business development. It rarely happens in one seren-dipitous exchange. So you need a system to make it work.

In 1999, I sought the advice of a career consultant. It was the one and only time in my life when I found myself needing to seek employment. Having spent a considerable amount of time working on my CV and my offering, he told me that he was going to help me with an 'aggressive marketing campaign'. I asked him what that meant. He replied, 'Going out to headhunters'. I asked him what sort of numbers, thinking he meant ten or fifteen. His answer astonished me: 'About four hundred'.

And we approached all of them. This was before email had really kicked in. His secretary prepared a stack of letters for me. I topped and tailed them, and sent them out, in batches of about twenty a day, over a month. The deal was simple. I was to call the headhunter, two days after the letter went out, to arrange a meeting.

To start with, this was like pulling teeth. The gate-keepers behaved like they might have done in a publishers' office if you were looking to get a book published. 'Thank you, we have your details on file, Mr Wood, and we'll call you as and when we have a search suitable for you'.

I had to utilise every last shred of charm in talking to these gate-keepers who had been programmed to keep me, and others like me, at bay. I simply said I would value a 20-minute cup of coffee with Peter So-and-So and would 11am next Tuesday, or the same time next Thursday, be more convenient?

More often than not, I got the appointments, and quite soon I landed a very interesting role as CEO of one of the top housing associations in the UK.

The lesson in persistence, which this process taught me, was simply without equal. Because, in the beginning, it is just so hard to deal with rejection, particularly if that rejection is of you, yourself, not just of some product or service that you might be offering. You learn, by persisting, to come to see what you are offering as having value—value that you genuinely want to share with the person you are talking to. As a gift. Shifting the paradigm from asking them for a favour, to giving them one. And then seeking to transact as equals. And learning that lesson has, quite simply, made a massive difference to my life. Just as it will to others who adopt the same strategy.

So, how can you adopt this strategy? It's simple:

1.  WRITE (Letter / Email / LinkedIn message)
2.  CALL
3.  MEET

Let's unravel this a bit more.

You start with reaching out. In 1999, for me, that was letters. An actual letter still goes a long way. But emails might be your best bet. And beyond that, all forms of other communications. You will need to decide, in each case, how you want to get to the enablers who you feel could benefit your business. I use LinkedIn a lot for this purpose. Others might find building online relationships through social media, or commenting on their blog posts, or saying something flattering about them in their own content, does the same job.

On LinkedIn, for example, I send a message to the person with whom I want to connect. I tell them in writing why I want to talk. I ask them for their help, and suggest what I might be able to do for them. That puts me under a little pressure to be succinct in what I am going to say. And perhaps also puts a little bit on them to help me.

I often write a letter to the person I want to connect with, typed on good quality writing paper, writing only on one side. Before you class me as a dinosaur, I freely acknowledge that letters are not common these days, but that is exactly why it works—precisely because it is both unusual and infrequent, it makes your approach stand out from the crowd. I set out, in the letter, who I am and what my mission is. Having researched my client's business, I refer to it and what I like about it. I may mention mutual contacts, when there are any, in an attempt to anchor us both on the same page. I then top and tail the letter in blue felt tip, in my own handwriting, and put it in a good quality envelope, write the name and address in the same blue felt tip, mark it, in capitals, strictly private and confidential, underline those words in red ink, put a first class stamp on it, and put it in the post. I make sure my letter gives the recipient my mobile number and email address, as I don't want to trouble them to have to write me a letter back!

I then follow up with an email two days later, when I am confident they will have received my letter, And, by then I will have been noticed. Writing well-constructed letters is a rarity these days, and makes a difference on its own.

Whatever form your written approach takes, it can be useful to suggest that you will call them at a certain time the following day. And then do just that. When you call you may get through to a secretary, PA, or assistant to of some kind, depending on the stature of the contact. I never ask for the contact to call me back, I simply find out when he or she is next expected to be around, and free, and ring back then, keeping the process going until I make contact. I do my best to charm the gatekeepers on the way through. It generally works.

From the outset of this call, I make the assumption that the other party will be willing to see me. I never ask them whether they will see me or not. I suggest a 20-minute chat over a cup of coffee, and I ask them which of two dates would suit them best, or whether they would like to suggest another time. I might even suggest a Zoom call instead, given how acceptable that has become at the current time.

This process is intended to pass on a little obligation to the contact to spare me a few minutes of their time. And it will also have shown me to be a little determined and persistent, which I find, so long as I have been polite as well, generally goes down OK with my targets, and can even impress them. You need to go into every meeting with the giving, not getting, mindset, particularly in the connected economy. It is an ethos of being of service. And you will see that, mostly, that mindset works.

# Negotiating

As with becoming good networkers, we need to become good negotiators too. There are many misconceptions about selling, and the same is true about negotiating. Many think that negotiating is about playing hardball, which is so rarely true. For a really successful negotiation, both sides must feel they have got a good deal.

We negotiate every single day—with family, to find a gap in the traffic, with the boss over time off, with friends over plans, when we buy a used car. For something we do so often, it makes sense for us to hone our skills. But who studies the subject? It is essential to do so.

The reason that hardball so rarely works in negotiation is because it does not promote creative thinking. Many would advise against making the first offer, but very often, to do so, can anchor the other party in the ball park you wish to be in.

Inexperienced negotiators often make the mistake of thinking that the key to negotiation lies in the numbers, but so often the real key can lie in other benefits, in satisfying emotional needs perhaps. Indeed, the other terms in any agreement can be balanced against the financial elements of that agreement. Always have a big list of items to go in the agreement: this is vital to any negotiation.

Really doing the homework, putting ourselves in the other party's shoes, thinking through all their alternatives, is essential to getting a good outcome. And have several outcomes in your mind—focussing on just one is often fatal.

Empathising with them lies at the very heart of getting the best deal.

Looking to grow the pie is also incredibly important to a successful outcome. It is so easy to see the other side as competition. Starting to think about joint problem solving is often the clue to the right outcome.

As is being authentic, revealing something about yourself. Behaving in a way where the other side feels they should reciprocate. Even be vulnerable. Ask 'If you were me, what would you ask for?'. Let the other side want to protect your position as well as theirs.

And never being afraid to walk away if you can see no alternative, once everything has been tried. So often it will put you in a stronger position.

Use negotiating tactics in emails. Using a 'No'-orientated question in the subject line to force your email to the top of the pile will make you come across as more authentic. Something like 'Have you decided to give up on X?' And then, end your email on a positive note, with a clear call to action: 'How does this sound?'

Starting nice, ending nice, and delivering harder messages in the middle. Keeping your eyes and ears open and looking and listening out for signals. Remembering that deadlines are usually fake.

All the above can be very useful tips when you find yourself in a tricky negotiation.

Think like the other side as much as you can. Too much introspection can let you down. Think: 'What do they need to get out of this to shake hands?'

Remember to actively communicate and actively listen at all times. Sometimes, just encourage silence by saying nothing. Active communication is the technique of communicating, both verbally and non-verbally, in a way that makes us agreeable and easy to understand. Active listening uses verbal and nonverbal cues—e.g. eye contact and nodding, alongside what we say, to show we are making a real effort to understand the other side and make it easier for them to trust us. Usually when someone gets a yes, they stop listening, and valuable information can then be lost into the ether. Remember that the meat of a conversation is not what comes out of our mouths, but what comes out of theirs. Be patient. Don't just trot out a solution—which so often makes us look too smart. And, use silence, as well as listening and being patient. It will bring us ever closer to the best outcome for us.

# Which 'A' Are You?

The finer skills of negotiation go way beyond the scope of this book, but, if you have an appetite to hone and improve your negotiating skills, then read Chris Voss' book, *Never Split The Difference*. Voss was a top hostage negotiator for the FBI before setting up the Black Swan Group to train individuals and companies in the art of negotiation. As a quick takeaway from Voss' training, he defines three personality types, into one, or more of which you and I both fall. These are:

- THE ASSERTIVE
- THE ANALYST
- THE ACCOMMODATOR

ASSERTIVES see themselves as honest, logical and direct. *Others see them as emotional, aggressive and harsh.*

ANALYSTS see themselves as realistic, prepared and smart. *Others see them as cold and stand offish.*

ACCOMMODATORS see themselves as personable, conversational and relationship focussed. *Others see them as Friendly and too talkative.*

Imagine you are assertive, and you are negotiating with an analyst. You've got your work cut out for you. Remember you only have a one in three chance of negotiating with a similar personality type. So, there is a lot to learn about communicating with people before even getting into the detail of negotiating techniques.

Resolving to get ever better at the joint arts of networking and negotiating will stand you in immensely good stead.

# A Note on Empathy

The importance of all of the above is that it doesn't work well without empathy. Forget war. Deal with war only if it is brought to your door. Try to make friends instead. Slow things down. We need to recognise that, for better or worse, we impact others. That impact can be negative, or it can be positive. We should aim for positive mutual impact in all our relationships. That way, both sides will benefit. And, the double bonus here is that this thinking leads to long term relationships not short-term gains. Negotiation is sometimes seen as a form of arm wrestling. It should not be. We need to change this mindset to one of thinking 'win, win, or no deal'.

# CHAPTER TEN

# MAPPING AND NAVIGATION

'Blue Sky Thinking' is a trite phrase. Most people think they know what it means. Very few know how to do it, or how to harvest the fruit that it yields.

A properly choreographed group session, with a facilitator to conduct it, is a place where creative ideas can be thrown in freely, once participants are assured that they will not be rubbished, and thus innovative infant plans can start to germinate.

For these sessions to be truly powerful, those engaging in them should practise by coming up with ten new ideas every day, as I suggested earlier in this book. The importance of coming up with ten new ideas a day, every single day, simply cannot be overestimated. When I suggest this to people, they usually say they think that might be excessive, and, indeed, wonder how such a large number of ideas could be useful. Once they have tried it, they generally change their minds.

# Ideas Generation

I said earlier in this book that entrepreneurs must become ideas machines. I come up with ten ideas every single day. It's really hard at first. But it gets almost ridiculously easy with practice. Some of my ideas—even most of them—are weak, occasionally even rubbish, but my ideas muscle has been massively exercised, and more and more ideas come, the more that I practise this. I recommend it to you very highly. It is ideas that will make you even more money than money itself, in the long run.

These ideas must be written down, so they are remembered, and there to review, and, if worthwhile, to develop. It may be that there is the kernel of something really interesting lurking in one of those ideas, and only by going back and reviewing those ideas do you find it.

Look at it this way. Somewhere, sometime, one of your ideas will be worth a million pounds. Perhaps a lot more. But if you don't keep coming up with new ideas, you won't find that golden nugget. Cultivating that ideas muscle is rather like beach combing, or opening oysters—your pearl is in there somewhere. And the more you beachcomb, the more pearls you find. It's just another percentage game. Just keep walking down the beach. Keep looking. Sometimes, we find ourselves in an arid wilderness—nothing creative seems to be in sight. But that is not the time to stop coming up with ideas—every single day. We can, and we must, generate that creativity.

Like an author must create his or her book. From scratch. We have to get the ball rolling. It's up to us. No freebies. Period.

Think about it. Ten minutes a day (maybe a bit more at first). Over the year, that is 3,650 ideas. Must be able to come up with a good one out of that, surely?

Once you and your team have got your ideas muscles working—just the same as getting your physical muscles working—it's time to get into group blue sky thinking.

The creative process is messy. Not a straight line from the original idea to the deliverable project. Very often some major changes of direction on the way—possibly even 180 degree turns.

Steven Pressfield's *The War of Art* highlights the forms of resistance faced by artists, entrepreneurs, athletes, and others who are trying to break through creative barriers. A book which is well worth the read.

# Running A Session

So, make sure you have a nice big whiteboard, on a strong stand. With working pens (not dried up ones!) to write on it with. Appoint one of your number as the facilitator to write down ideas, act as coach and develop subjects. Remember that, in a lockdown or post-lockdown world, Zoom comes with its own effective 'Whiteboard' function.

There are no rules for the session, except this one. No negative ideas. Only positive ones can be written down. Rubbishing anyone's ideas is the quickest possibly way to kill off their creative flow. So never do it. Always nurture them instead.

Start the session when everybody is fresh. When you all have at least an hour to spare. No interruptions are allowed—no texts, no emails, no phone calls. Time it and stop when you get to the end of the hour.

I generally start these sessions with a few questions to get the mental juices flowing, and anchor things in a place where we are now. Here are some ideas:

1. What were our biggest achievements in the last twelve months?
2. Where did we waste most time in that period?
3. What has taken up most of our time in that period?
4. Where have our best clients come from during that time, and why are they the best?

You will get the idea—these questions are simply here to catalyse the process and get it going. Thinking is the hardest work we ever do—so let's make it fun—supporting each other as we come up with the best of it.

I am ALWAYS amazed by the creativity. The sheer number of ideas. And the power of the cross pollination.

When you are done, the facilitator takes a photo of the whiteboard on their Phone (or screenshots the

Zoom board), and then wipes it clean. His, or her, duty is complete when the notes have been sorted, typed up and circulated to the team, for comment and review, prior to the next session.

Enjoy it. It's fun, and it will make you money.

Businesses are a bit like little seeds, which will hopefully grow. At the beginning, the seed of an idea is formed. It is planted. If it is watered and nurtured and exposed to sunlight, it should start to grow. But as it is tested by tough conditions, it may wither. There will be other ideas, one of which will start to grow up strongly. Sometimes the strongest growers started off as uninspiring weaklings. While most seeds will not become big plants or trees, some will, and it will often be up to the inspiration and efforts of those who are nurturing them, which ensure that they grow into adolescence, or even mature into adulthood.

Good planning will play a very important part. So, will determination. A refusal to give up. Support from others. Luck. A combination of all the above.

Once ideas have been harvested and approved as worthwhile by the team, they need to be fed into forward planning with some kind of timescale. They may need further investigation—a task which could be allocated to a team member. They may need to go on the back burner with a future date for their review. But, what must not happen, is to let them die there due to lack of implemention. And make sure, whatever action is allocated to each idea, that it is followed up at the time agreed for that purpose.

# CHAPTER ELEVEN

# THE SHAPE OF YOUR FLIGHT

(I suddenly noticed that, by pure coincidence, this chapter—Chapter 11—just happened to be the point where this book was ready to deal with changes in business fortunes. Chapter 11, for those who do not know it, is a form of bankruptcy in America. I chose not to change the chapter!)

Watch any aircraft and you notice the shifts up and down, the lefts and rights—subtle of course, seen from below, but crucial inputs the pilot must make to maintain steady flight and keep on course. Movements that may be necessitated by weather conditions. It is, of course, the same in your business. You may find more turbulence on your journey than you would like.

In this chapter we will anatomise the likely life cycles of your business—including its end, whether that's climbing to higher altitudes or simply trying to avoid a crash. And either avoiding it—or not.

The lifecycle of a business from infancy to adolescence and maturity—and, sometimes, senescence—is something we have touched on before in discussions about the Technician, the Manager and the Entrepreneur. It must be at the core of your own diagnostic understanding. Businesses in their infancy are indistinguishable from their owner. Businesses reaching adolescence will start to show signs of separation between ownership and management. And businesses, in their maturity, will start to show a greater degree of independence between ownership and management. Very often, at the mature stage, founders will spend more time working ON the business rather than IN it. There are some generalisations here, but this will serve as a broad guide.

# Infancy

In the early years of a business, much experimentation will go on. A lot of learning. A game of snakes and ladders with a good amount of both. Trying things out. Seeing what works and what doesn't. Perhaps, at the beginning, as a sole trader before putting on corporate clothing. Any finance at this point will usually have come from family, maybe from good friends as well. It is unlikely that outsiders will have come in to help financially yet. The business will stand or fall on how it fares in this early stage, before it grows up and moves on to Adolescence.

# Adolescence

Adolescence, in a business, usually comes when employees are added. Maybe where outside advice is sought. The business is still finding its feet, but it is starting to make an important distinction between the individual and the business—which are largely one and the same in the infant stage—and the two are now beginning to become more separate. The proprietor realises he cannot do it all—products, services, customers, marketing, finance, delivery, administration etc.—and must either stay as a small one-man band or add others to enable growth. Indicators of adolescence include:

- Hiring. Some experimentation will be taking place here, as these may well be the first people you've ever employed. You will need to learn how to train, supervise and support them. It's a big ask from someone who has never done it before. Even choosing that first employee or two is a lottery.

- Systems, embryonic ones at least, will have been put into place, so you can organise how things work.

- You may have established more formal branding and marketing. Once again, this will be a question of trial and error.

- You may have brought in the first outside investor or two. These will want quite a lot of information on which to base their decision to invest, and they will want a reasonable (or sometimes unreasonable) slice of the pie to persuade them to take a risk on such a very early stage investment. See *Dragon's Den* for examples of this.

So, lots more moving parts are in play now than was the case in the infancy of the business, and there is a lot more to go wrong. This is the moment when a lot of businesses fail. A moment for cool heads, and for knowing what you are doing. A time, most certainly, for a critical friend and trusted advisor to hold your feet to the fire and speak in very plain language.

## Maturity

For the businesses that survive Adolescence, there is now a moment for a little cautious self-congratulation. To get through Infancy and Adolescence takes quite some doing, a big element of multi-tasking, tackling situations (maybe new ones never encountered before) which will require a lot of good judgement and a very cool head. But arguably things get even harder now, and you'll have even greater responsibility.

What signs will you see to show you are entering the Mature stage? Some of the list below are useful indications of this point:

- Employees
- A business plan
- A brand and a marketing plan
- Financial controls
- Some systems
- Some trading results
- Some profits

In a nutshell: we are still around. So, we want to grow again.

Some formality is now needed. Some regular reporting of results, to both investors and bankers. Greater financial sophistication—perhaps a full-time financial accountant. Employee formality is increasing, bringing with it the need for some HR rules. Perhaps even a non executive director or two. Some management of risk. Thoughts being given to a sale at some point in the future.

## Beyond Maturity

You made it into adulthood, but of course, as we know for ourselves, life doesn't stop at 18. Never forget that maturity is still only the START. The end of the beginning.

But, hopefully not the beginning of the end! As, the business gets bigger, the opportunities and responsibilities will continue to expand. The business will ALWAYS have challenges, ALWAYS have needs. These will be constantly changing, like the weather, due to competition and the micro and macro economic climates affecting the business. It is your job to be the mountain guide—to think several steps ahead of the business, as it continues on its journey, so as to be prepared, often with a plan B, or even a plan C, to cope with any unexpected eventualities.

And remember this. No business EVER reaches some utopian summit, where it can remain static, forever, in a state of perfection. Such a state does not exist. As Bob Dylan wrote, so accurately 'he, not busy being born, is busy dying'. It's the same for businesses as for people. Keeping a business in balance for the rest of its life is the key role of its owners, its chairman and its CEO. They can sell it. Or the shareholders can pass the baton of responsibility to other professional managers. But never think, for one moment, that this responsibility will EVER end. The vagaries of markets, and the behaviour of people, make that no more than a pipe dream. If you don't believe me, consider, in the not so distant past, the futures (or lack of them) for companies like Thomas Cook, Polaroid, Kodak, Blackberry, Yellow Pages, Woolworths and House of Fraser who failed to read the tea leaves in time.

# The Midlife Review

Note I said 'review' and not 'crisis' here. For a business in good hands, the development beyond maturity will not be triggered by a crisis. But it is certainly the time when solid reflection is needed. This is where a lot of the things we have explored so far come in to play. Consult your accountant and reflect on the patterns and projections of numbers to date. Revisit your marketing strategy and keep adapting it, to keep it alive. Consider your flight crew—who do you need to add (or lose)? Consider your range of products and services. Think about how your business is run. Perhaps there are changes you'd like to make to your own quality of life now.

Things might be going well, but they can always go better. And, there may be someone, better suited than you, to take over the helm at this point. There's always more sky to accommodate your craft.

When you conduct this review, be entirely realistic. It is all too often the case that leaders wrongly identify what stage of the life cycle they are in. How many times on Dragons' Den do you see people go away empty-handed, knowing that if they had waited a year, or gone a year earlier, they'd have been successful? You have to remember when to change gear.

# End of Life Challenges

Other changes happen in companies during their lives. The Midlife Review might trigger thoughts of radically changing the business. We must not shy away from thinking about this, and it is important to be prepared.

Generally, a company might change at this point in one of the following ways:

# Handing Over The Wheel

Ownership of companies may change, subtly or majorly, on quite a regular basis. The original thinking, when joint stock companies were first conceived, was that they would provide a mechanism to separate the owners of a business from its managers. In larger companies, especially quoted ones, this works very well, and enables shareholders to dispose of their shares, in full or in part, quickly and easily, without the need to change management.

In a smaller private company, where there is no quoted market for shares, ownership tends to change hands much more slowly, although investor encouragement through the EIS and SEIS schemes has produced a new brand of shareholders—usually less loyal and long term than the founders—who invest with a view to a profitable exit in the short to medium term. This category would also include the providers of private equity venture capital, with whom you should only engage using extreme caution and considerable due diligence.

For unlimited partnerships, and, to some extent, limited liability partnerships, there is a less clear path to disposal, due to the absence of share capital. But it can still be done if a willing buyer can be found.

In addition, there are occasions in the life of almost every company when the owners want to change ownership, or where they are forced out, or agree to separate, because of incompatibility (which might have come about through changing attitudes over the passage of time, or which might have been there from the outset due to lack of proper due diligence—I have referred to this below).

These situations tend to lead to:

- MANAGEMENT BUY OUTS, where a manager, or a group of managers, want to buy out the owners because their circumstances have changed. The owners may be another company whose directors have decided that this company no longer fits into their future plans, or founder/owners who want to move on—to retire or turn their focus to other things.

- MANAGEMENT WALK OUTS, or situations where management is kicked out—these circumstances herald the need for new managers, and the best way to find them may be to dispose of all or some of the shares to those new managers to provide them with the necessary incentives.

- BUSINESS DIVORCE, where the working owners have a major falling out over how the business should be run. This generally means, if their differences cannot be resolved, that one, or some, will buy the other/others out.

- SUCCESSION TO A NEW GENERATION, the norm in most family-owned businesses, where the new generation must be brought on to the point where it is safe to give them, or sell them, the keys to the business. This will usually be delicate and sensitive. The younger generation may think that they know better, while the older one may know they don't! There will usually have to be a period of managed handover, and trusted advisors will play an essential part here.

These can be tricky times for companies. Times when eyes can get taken off the ball. Opinions differ as to how exits should be engineered and over how long a period of time. And at what value. The critical lesson to learn from the fact that these events occur in the normal course of the life of a business is that preparations must be in place to deal with them when they do. In essence, this means the equivalent of a prenuptial agreement to govern the rights and responsibilities of both share-holders and management. This means having a carefully thought through shareholders' agreement, together with service contracts for the directors.

## Going Separate Ways

I regularly deal with cases where directors or partners in a business want to separate. One, in the view of the other, may have been lazy, stupid, dishonest, unreliable, failed to pull their weight, or whatever. Maybe, worse, they are alleged to have been in breach of their fiduci-ary duty. And then we discover, with horror, that there is a complete lack of any kind of paperwork to document any of this.

So, the divorce that inevitably ensues has no rules to govern it. Each of the partner directors own 50%. There is no prearranged agreement to deal with the sale and pur-chase of shares, or the liquidation of the company, or to obtain any other redress. And so, advisors are brought in. Mediation takes place to try and resolve the protagonists' differences. And fees (which can be quite high) start to roll up. And all entirely avoidable, with the proper docu-mentation in place from the outset.

In essence, there needs to be an agreement to gov-ern the sale and purchase of shares, or the liquidation of the company. Otherwise there is deadlock. And quite possibly litigation. This is a time when a critical friend or trusted advisor can work to help the parties to try to resolve matters as amicably as possibly. The best advisor will be one who is trusted by all parties and capable of maintaining discretion about what each party tells him, or her. Negotiating skills will be essential. And access to other wise advisors.

The eventual outcome will be heavily dependent on fairness and open handedness between the parties. These are tricky and sensitive times for companies, and they must be treated as such. The long-term success of such changes will rely heavily on how well-planned and executed they were.

## Buying Not Starting

In addition to the above changes of ownership must be added the situation where an entrepreneur decides to buy a business, rather than starting one from scratch. This is a bigger subject than this book can accommodate, but it is an interesting one to consider. In addition, an existing business owner might decide to buy a competitor, supplier or client company to accelerate the growth of the existing organisation, or, perhaps, to merge with one. This process will require expert help, and forensic due diligence.

# Rewarding other participants

Maybe you want to give shares to those who act, in some way, or other, as partners in a business. A rule of thumb might be to reward people in roughly equal proportions, for example ⅓ for the owners, ⅓ for the team and ⅓ to reinvest for the growth of the company. People to consider here might be:

- Those who had the business idea
- Those who manage the business
- Those who raise the money
- Those who bring in the revenues
- Those who build the product
- Those who perform the services

# The Midlife Crisis

Yes, I did use the word crisis. Sometimes it will be the case. You know your business is in trouble. There's no option for a change in ownership. What choices are you left with? Generally they fall into the 'Three Rs': Reboot, Reorganisation, Rescue. There's a fourth R too. But we'll come to that later on. It might not be possible to see, from the inside, what you need. Again, this is where your trusted advisor comes in.

# Reboot

Usually this comes when a company stalls after a period of lack lustre performance, market difficulties, team bonding issues or general loss of direction. In a nutshell, under focussed exhaustion. A situation which sometimes can, in the simplest cases, be remedied by changing course by only a few degrees. Motivation and encouragement will be the key ingredients needed here. But, equally, there will almost certainly be some tough decisions needed—these may well include removing blocks, which might include key people who may have been responsible for causing the business to stall. This is always an event which should trigger a major white board session between the key players, as well as getting an outside trusted advisor to interview EVERY member of the team, to ask them four key questions:

- What they think is wrong about the organisation?
- What they think is right about it?
- What they think needs changing? And
- What part would they like to play in that change?

Answers from that exercise can be very revealing. Before new plans are put in place, and action taken to carry them out, the key team should meet with the outside trusted advisor to reach consensus on the future plan before enacting it.

# Reorganisation

A Reorganisation is usually brought about when a company failed to get a Reboot and the situation became chronic. A reorganisation is a more extreme version of a Reboot, and a less extreme one than a Rescue. It, like a Reboot, is usually not potentially terminal. Treatment will be largely the same as for a Reboot, but more extreme. To understand this better, it is worth revisiting earlier chapters on the original construction of a business. Layers of the business, which are not working, may need to be removed in order to streamline its processes.

# Rescue

By far and away the most serious situation that a business can face, short of entering receivership or going into liquidation, is the need for a rescue. This is usually, but not always, brought on by serious cash strictures. A company can still be profitable, but if it runs out of cash, the party is usually over—and quickly. The trouble with this kind of situation is that a solution usually needs to be found very quickly. Time is not on the company's side. Things have been allowed to unravel, and finding help, at times like these, is especially difficult because it involves negotiating a rescue from a position of weakness, not from one of strength.

The problems here will usually have been brought on by falling turnover or cost over runs. Possibly, because of over optimism, a situation which could have been resolved, from a position of relative strength a few months earlier, has now become desperate.

Unless there is a strong, even if illiquid, asset base, additional borrowing will usually not be an option, except at usurious rates, which are the last thing that a company, finding itself in this position, will want or need.

So, additional equity is often the only way out. Although that is not always easy to attract, if the situation is very difficult, because the idea of investing equity is to make a profit, and in these circumstances it will not always be easy to see profits on the horizon. Even if they can be seen, albeit dimly, equity will usually come at a very expensive price and, often, with extra strings attached.

On these occasions, rising panic is usually the first thing to be dealt with. At a time when it is hard to stay calm. But where calm is vital for the correct thinking which might lead to salvation. A well-connected critical friend and trusted advisor can be a real godsend at these moments—knowing what to do, in what order, who to call, what to say, how to negotiate and a host of other things, including getting the unvarnished facts as a precursor to the above.

It is easy for the proprietors to give up and throw in the towel. They should absolutely not do that, unless, and until, every single other avenue has been explored first.

The darkest hour is so often the one that comes before the dawn. And, if such a situation is turned around, and the company put back on a sound footing, then it will be all the stronger for that, and the cloud of the preceding crisis may well turn out to have had an inbuilt silver lining.

# Receivership

There is a fourth R. It's the one that drove me to write this book. Sometimes, all other ways exhausted, there is simply no way out. It starts with the appointment of a Receiver & Administrator—whose role is to try and get the business back on its feet again, and return it to the control of the directors, or sell all, or part of it, to either existing management or a third party. A 'Prepack' can be used to do this—a sale and purchase agreement is prepared, a purchaser having been found. The company goes into administration, and immediately, the new purchaser signs the sale and purchase agreement, allowing seamless trading between the old company and the new. This avoids pressure from creditors, and the cost of the administrator trading in the business. Prepacks have, from time to time, attracted negative press—especially where they have not been handled professionally. The point is to rescue the company as a going concern, to achieve a better result for the company's creditors than if the company were wound up, or to release property to make a distribution to secured or preferential creditors. The process must be run transparently.

All of these situations will need the help of an outside trusted advisor and mentor, capable, not only of providing calming and wise advice, but also knowing who to talk to, what professionals to get involved, so as to ensure that the solution, and future plan, has the greatest possible chance of being robust and successful, and looks like it might have a long shelf life.

Whether it is rebooting, reorganising, rescuing, or putting the company into receivership, seeking wise, independent advice, at the earliest possible moment, has the potential to vastly increase the chances of pulling off a successful outcome.

# CHAPTER TWELVE

# SURVIVING A CRASH LANDING

'I am strong because I have been weak. I am fearless because I have been afraid. I am wise because I have been foolish. I can laugh, because I have known sadness' (Anon). This lovely quote encapsulates the moment when the entrepreneur has failed, and must get up, dust himself or herself off, and start again.

To the true entrepreneur, this moment, in some form or other, will always come. For some, many times. It may come as a curse, or it may come as a blessing. It usually starts as the former, and turns into the latter. And, strange though it may sound, you must welcome it, because it is part of your growth.

It is a moment for serious reflection. 'Too painful,' you say. Yes, but if we want to grow, this is the only way forward.

You have come up with an idea. You have set up your business. You have not only put your money into it, but also hours and hours and hours of your time. You have created your product or service. Built up a good customer base. Taken on employees. Tried with all your might to keep it going during a downturn in the market. Run out of cash. And had to close it down.

Sometimes, you can let go of a company in such a way that it parachutes gently down to a soft landing. You can pay the creditors. Or someone wants to take it off your hands.

On other occasions, you crash land. Less happiness all around. Sometimes, you can walk away. Sometimes, you are a stretcher case. That's just the reality.

Be philosophical. Just like landings in an aircraft, all landings are good landings if you exit them alive, without too much collateral damage.

Up the ladder. Down the snake. The occupational hazards of entrepreneurship.

## Letting Yourself Heal

Once you have let the business go, you will need to recover damaged confidence. Learn the lessons it has offered you. Move on. This is just so hard. To convince yourself that you can succeed again. Trying to count up—and revalue—your dented skills and battered experience. Putting your wet boots back on, and getting back out on that long cold road again.

In becoming a successful entrepreneur, maintaining

sanity, and a good work/life balance, is beyond essential. It will make the difference between real success, of the rounded kind, where family and friends play truly important parts in your life, and you succeed in business nevertheless—and the less satisfactory state of affairs where your business is a huge success, but that success comes at a price (which should be truly unaffordable) of divorce, cold relationships with family, a dearth of friends, ill health and so on.

Use the time after parting from your business to remember what's important and let that heal you while you lick your wounds. We have families and friends who love us, and want, and deserve, to be awarded some of our time and attention. If we devote all of it to our business interests, at their expense, how can we say, hand on heart, that we have truly succeeded?

Therefore, maintaining a healthy work life balance is so hugely important. Missing kids' matches and plays comes at one hell of a cost. And you can't bottle those up and enjoy them later. They are gone for all time. To repent about at your leisure. Just not worth the pain.

Read. I have recommended a lot of books in my writing here. Books remind us that we are not alone. Others have certainly made bigger mistakes than you and bounced back from them. Listen to stories of failure and success. Let them remind you that this is a natural part of business life. Through this, you will change your mind set about what has happened. Remove the shame and disappointment. You will start to see that failure is a powerful and positive thing in itself. And, one that should be truly celebrated.

# Celebrate Your Failure

As you will remember from the preface to this book, I had a very hard landing in November 2012. Personal bankruptcy was the consequence of the unwinding of a large property portfolio, following the credit squeeze of 2008.

Aside from having practically no cash at all, I had no capital, no credit rating (and thus no chance of getting credit) and a deep sense of guilt that I could probably have avoided this outcome had I concentrated properly, read the tea leaves, and sold the portfolio earlier. Avoided my own fate, and an identical one for my wife, who was an innocent party, taken down with me simply because her name was on a lot of the property deeds. And, just to make matters even more tricky, I was 61 at the time.

The stigma attaching to bankruptcy in the UK is odd. America has a much healthier attitude. It sees it as a rite of passage. The British also have a strange attitude to failure. Strange, because failure is just so essential to success. Failure leads to ultimate success for the persistent, persevering, entrepreneur. So, in a nutshell, there need be no failures. Why? Because, the only true failure is when we give up. And, that, we don't do, do we? Life, especially business, is a bit like playing Snakes and Ladders. We can try to control events, but, even then, we will find ourselves, from time to time, at the foot of a Snake. Embrace it. It will teach you a lot more than the ladders.

As I said in the preface, this event, nevertheless, was one of the best in my life. However, a little while after, I had a health scare due to the years of stress. I collapsed on a ferry to France. Paramedics scrambled and serious thought was given to turning the ferry round and returning to Dover. Happily, it remained headed for France, and, I suspect that I got better treatment from the hospital in Calais than I would have done in Dover.

I gave up coffee and alcohol from that moment, and have drunk neither since. I changed my diet, started taking exercise, getting at least eight hours quality sleep every night, and studiously avoiding stress. I started to feel better than I had felt for years. Building endorphins (to handle pain), oxytocin (through being sociable), serotonin (to stay cheerful) and dopamine (to look forward).

I decided to cut back on my possessions. Reduce clutter. Create a simpler life. It has made my powers of concentration so much better.

And I began to focus on the details of business like I never had before. I set up Runway Advisors as a collective to help entrepreneurs to make more money and have more fun doing it. My role has been, and still is, to act as Critical Friend and Trusted Advisor to a wide range of small-to-medium-sized enterprises, operating in a broad variety of different fields. I could not have even begun to do this had I not had the experiences I have set out above. Building on those foundations, I have added, at the time of writing, other professional advisors who help support our clients in their specific discipline.

And I became an author. I am now deeply involved in writing and publishing a number of books, including this one. I have a long list of subjects to cover. The next one is the first in a series of five thrillers. I have all five book covers ready, so I cannot wimp out.

I very much doubt if you will face as hard a landing as I did, and, as I hope I have shown, you can still walk away from it—and prosper.

## Picking Yourself Back Up

If you're a dyed in the wool entrepreneur, when your cuts and bruises heal, you'll have a new idea, a regenerated belief in yourself, in your abilities, in your contacts and you'll start another business. Remember, each new business idea has to start right back with those foundations again. Come up with your idea and repeat all the first chapters in the book. Somewhere along the line—in that process—you will get something right that was wrong before. And, remember, you will need to have the wind in your sails. And, don't be surprised, if it isn't there at first. Keep your eyes open. Watch and wait like a sniper.

And seize opportunities as they come.

> Still, around the corner, there may wait
> A new road, or a secret gate
> And, 'though we pass by them today
> Tomorrow, we may come this way
> And, take the hidden paths that run
> Towards the moon—or to the sun

Return to all those daily idea lists you generated. Bat about ideas with someone from your old team that you trust and who knows you well. Find those gaps in the market where you could innovate and thrive. Find that passion again. See how, and where, you might find your fuel. Remember that everyone dies, but not everyone lives. You can always make your money back. But you can never get one minute of your time back.

You might have to set up twenty businesses to come up with your big success. How many people fall in love with, and stay happily married to, the first person they meet? You probably have, and if you have, you judged better first time over than I did.

# Can Entrepreneurship Be a Job for Life?

Happily, entrepreneurship is a lifelong love affair with all its ups and downs. Steve Jobs said it was hard to join up the dots looking forwards; that you could only do it by looking backwards, to find the pattern that was always there.

Just remember, not one of us gets to leave this planet alive. So, get out there and have a ball. Think not 'What if?' but 'What next?'. It's time to get out on today's journey.

We all need to enjoy the journey. In the aftermath of corona virus, we need to think more than before about our health. My plan is to live to be at least 100 years young, and never retire. To die young and healthy at a very advanced age.

You are invited to my 100th Birthday party, in 2051. But, to avoid disappointment at the door, please do not bring sticks, Zimmer frames or wheelchairs, because they get in the way of the dancing.

To get there, I am trying to observe the rules of *Ikagai*:

- To remain active and never retire
- To leave urgency behind
- To eat until I am 80% full
- To surround myself only with good, positive friends
- To keep myself in shape with gentle exercise every single day

- To smile and acknowledge others
- To reconnect with nature
- To give thanks for anything that brightens up my day and makes me feel more alive
- To live in the moment, &
- To follow my *ikagai*—curiosity

What is your reason for jumping out of bed in the morning? How will you follow your own *ikagai?*

I wish you the very best luck in the world on your own journey. I hope that, even if only in just one small way, this book may help you to avoid a few of the pitfalls which are hard wired into this territory.

Safe travels—and keep smiling.

# BUILDING YOUR OWN RUNWAY

I have supported a wide variety of companies in a wide variety of ways over the past 40, or more, years, but my overarching mission has remained the same throughout: to help more businesses make more money, and have more fun doing it.

Real change happens when a real connection is made, and that means getting to know clients' businesses intimately, becoming a trusted part of the inner workings. I am not a consultant, working by the hour, on the touchline, out of the cut and thrust of the game. I am an advisor, on the pitch, working with the team, rooting for them to win. There is a world of difference.

I specialise in helping clients to navigate moments of change or crisis. There is nothing more rewarding than supporting companies who feel 'stuck' to identify and overcome obstacles and grow. I am non-sector specific, moving across all sectors, remaining objective, and getting to the pith of what needs to be done quickly.

Working with start-ups and entrepreneurs is particularly fulfilling. Every fledgling company needs every possible source of help and back-up from the get-go, to make it in a hostile marketplace.

Entrepreneurs drive change, make the world better, and largely do it all on their own, at their own risk, running on their own passion. They are the great unsung heroes. I know from my own long entrepreneurial career what the obstacles and potholes are. I love to share with my clients the escape routes out of difficulty, which I have learnt the hard way, and how to maximise them to ensure both survival and growth. How to replace losing strategies with winning ones.

As a generalist, I have built a network of go-to experts, over the years, to offer clients specialist support. Things work better when we work together. And so, in 2018, Runway Advisors was born. By connecting with me, you are connecting with a one-stop shop of support. I love networking, and forming teams, collaborating with others. Bringing together different areas of expertise to cover off every base. To balance up my weaknesses by adding in others' strengths, and vice versa. We watch each others' backs, mentor and care for each other. Everyone needs that. Working situations are complex. Better solved by a combination of skills. By a team.

Runway Advisors was set up to do exactly this. While I understand business strategy, financial planning, mentoring, mediating, negotiating, troubleshooting, critical friendship and so on, I have no deep knowledge of recovery and insolvency, taxation, legal matters or company secretarial duties. The same is true of investment management. I am also pretty ignorant on investigations and risk. And, I am not much better on performance coaching or, HR, for that matter. Finally, I need much help from others to understand the inner workings of marketing, communications, editorial, branding, design, social media or digital marketing. And IT.

Runway Advisors come together as a group which is available, in fractions, to a wide range of clients. We hope to bring mutual impact to those clients, and be to their enterprises, a net profit, NEVER a net cost. If we cannot be the former, then we should not be there at all.

So, instead, I collaborate. And stop worrying about my weaknesses. I benefit. My colleagues benefit. Even more importantly, so do our clients. We work to make them feel safe.

I strongly recommend that you focus on building your team. For stronger collaboration and networking. And, yes, for more fun. Let me know if you think we can help you.

**www.runwayadvisors.co.uk**

' It's not the critic who counts; not the man who points out how the strong man stumbles, or where the doer of deeds could have done them better. The credit belongs to the man (or woman) who is actually in the arena, whose face is marred by dust and sweat and blood; who strives valiantly; who errs, who comes short again and again, because there is no effort without error and shortcoming; but who does actually strive to do the deeds; who knows great enthusiasms, the great devotions; who spends himself in a worthy cause; who at the best knows, in the end, the triumph of high achievement, and who at the worst, if he fails, at least fails while daring greatly, so that his place shall never be with those cold and timid souls who neither know victory nor defeat.'

Theodore Roosevelt

# Business Diagnostics

A compilation of the questions and exercises suggested throughout the book, to make your thinking, planning and auditing more efficient. Remember to turn to these diagnostic tools regularly throughout your business journey. Always be completely honest, completely accurate and completely open-minded.

# Which 'A' Are You?

Inspired by *Never Split the Difference* by Chris Voss

| | 1<br>YES | 2<br>MAYBE | 3<br>NO |
|---|---|---|---|
| I am a rational thinker | | | |
| I root things in fact | | | |
| I am honest in my opinions | | | |
| I am direct with people | | | |
| People sometimes say I am too harsh | | | |
| Some people say I am aggressive | | | |
| My emotions can sometimes get in the way of business | | | |

### SCORE

10 or below ——————————— You are an 'ASSERTIVE'

10–15 ——————————— You are an 'ANALYST'

15 or above ——————————— You are an 'ACCOMMODATOR'

|  | 1<br>YES | 2<br>MAYBE | 3<br>NO |
|---|---|---|---|
| A happy business is a good business |  |  |  |
| People say I am very warm and friendly |  |  |  |
| I get on well with everyone I work with |  |  |  |
| Sometimes people say I talk too much |  |  |  |
| The best thing about work is the people |  |  |  |
| I know most of my clients/customers by name |  |  |  |
| Meetings I am in often run on longer than expected |  |  |  |

**SCORE**

10 or below _____ You are an 'ASSERTIVE'

10–15 _____ You are an 'ANALYST'

15 or above _____ You are an 'ACCOMMODATOR'

|  | I<br>YES | 2<br>MAYBE | 3<br>NO |
|---|---|---|---|
| I love planning |  |  |  |
| All problems can be avoided by good preparation |  |  |  |
| You don't need to be friends with the people you work with |  |  |  |
| I am smarter than most people I know |  |  |  |
| Some people might say I'm too negative or critical, but I'm just being realistic |  |  |  |

### SCORE

10 or below ————————————————You are an 'Assertive'

10–15 ————————————————You are an 'Analyst'

15 or above ——————————You are an 'Accommodator'

# The Kipling Questions

The who, what, where, when, why, how survey of your business idea. The third column is empty for your responses.

| | | |
|---|---|---|
| **WHAT** | What business are you setting up? | |
| | What will it sell? | |
| | What do you want out of it? | |
| | What will you do with it when it is built? | |
| | What are your strong skills? | |
| | What are you less good at? | |
| | What do you need to take out of it while you are building it? | |
| **WHY** | Are you setting it up to give you a strong financial future? | |
| | Is the business an interesting sideline for you? | |
| | Do you eventually want to sell it? | |
| | Will you keep it in the family? | |

| | | |
|---|---|---|
| **WHEN** | When are you going to start it? | |
| | When will it be built? | |
| | When will you hire others to help you? | |
| | When will it be 'finished'—ready to keep or sell? | |
| **HOW** | How are you going to build it? | |
| | How are you going to finance it? | |
| **WHERE** | Where are you going to operate it from? | |
| | Where are you going to source your products, services? | |
| | Where will you find customers and clients? | |
| **WHO** | Who will your fellow architects be? | |
| | Who is the entrepreneur? | |
| | Who is the technician? | |
| | Who is the manager? | |
| | Who else is going to be working with you? | |
| | Who will you get to advise you—both on business strategy and on finance? | |

# Diagnosing Stuckness

- What you need to be an entrepreneur
- The big idea for your product or service
- The plan for your business—do you know where you are and want to be in three years?
- Managing your finances—are your costs under control? Is your pricing right?
- Dealing with people—have you the right mix of skills? The right advisors?
- Branding and marketing—are you happy with how sales and prospecting are going?
- Creating systems and processes
- Networking—how are your contacts? Are you a good connector?
- Negotiating—are you a good negotiator?
- Refreshing your thinking
- Developing the business further
- How to deal with succession
- How to reboot, rescue or reorganise the business— and if all else fails, how to start again

# Are You In The Right Aircraft?

Whether you've launched your business or not, these key questions below must be asked. It's possible to be a gifted pilot, an intuitive navigator, and still be in the wrong kind of plane.

- Is it scalable?
- Are the local demographics favourable?
- Have you a brand in mind? Have you worked on it? Asked people what they think of it?
- Is it visually strong, catchy, memorable?
- Could you see it attracting a big network of support?
- Better still, could you be creating a monopoly— even if only a local one? The only ferry to the island?

# Competitor Analysis

Assess the landscape of your business specialism or offering. Ask yourself the following questions as you conduct your competitor research:

- What does your competition consist of?
- How do their offerings compare to yours?
- How are their offerings structured?
  Do they have different levels?
- What makes them different from you?
- How does the pricing compare with yours?
- How well-funded are they?
- How are they finding customers?
- What branding and copy are they using?
- What makes them special?
- What can you learn from them?
- Is it possible to co-exist?
- Is there any potential for collaboration?

# The 25 Key Questions

Make sure you think about and answer the following questions when constructing your business plan...

1. How good are your margins?
2. Where do you manufacture your product?
3. How easily can it be produced?
4. How many could you sell in the first three years?
5. How much stock would you need to hold?
6. What are the strengths of the product or service?
7. If appropriate, is it patented?
8. What are its weaknesses?
9. What opportunities does it bring?
10. What threats are linked to it?
11. How unique is it?
12. What is the quality of it? (a lot more important than its price)
13. Is anything similar on offer at the moment? And at what price? And is it succeeding?
14. How well received has it been?
15. How big is the demand?
16. How good are the margins?
17. How fashionable/seasonal is it?
18. How much capital is it likely to take to achieve that?
19. What size premises would you need?
20. What staffing would you need?
21. What equipment would you need?

22. Where are you going to get the money, if needed, and on what terms?
23. What the business will look like when it is done;
24. When it will be done; and
25. What you are going to do with it once it is done.

# IBM Visioning

- What will your company look like?
- How would that vision of a company need to act?
- How can you act that way from the beginning?

# People Skills Audit

Consider each of the essential elements below and score yourself and others on a scale of 1 to 3 to identify your internal resource.

| QUALITY | NAME OF PERSON | 1. NO SKILL | 2. SOME SKILLS | 3. VERY SKILLED |
|---|---|---|---|---|
| People/Team building | | | | |
| Marketing | | | | |
| Selling | | | | |
| Negotiation | | | | |
| Finance | | | | |
| Administration | | | | |
| Strategy (conception) | | | | |
| Operations (execution) | | | | |
| Tech/ systems | | | | |

# Defining Your Business

1. Write down all the things your business does.
2. Now write down everything your business **is**—your overall ethos, what world you want to create, what stories you want to tell. What makes you unique.
3. How did you begin? Tell us the story of how you came to exist as a business.
4. Write 'We believe' several times down the side of your page and complete the mission statements.
5. Pick all your best sentences from above and edit them into one page. Use headings if you like. Lots of businesses find it useful to have a bullet point mission statement of sorts.
6. Now turn this into one paragraph.
7. Now reduce it down to a single sentence. Try it out on a few people. Do they understand it? Do you understand it? Is it really what you want to say?

# Also from Ed Wood

**Plague of Madness**
Collected here, a year after the Covid-19 outbreak began, Wood's diary entries offer a compelling, real-time chronology of Britain's handling of the pandemic, political developments and observations on the economy, alongside his own increasingly vitriolic and desperate reflections, as he watches his country bounce recklessly from 'common sense into common madness'.

Data and government soundbites sit alongside haircuts, trampolining, Orwell, Dad's Army, poetry, music (and futuristic pizza ordering) in this kaleidoscopic summary of twelve wildly unprecedented months.

Publication date: 30<sup>th</sup> May 2021

What people have said about *Plague Of Madness*

'I am truly alarmed at the speed with which my fellow citizens willingly suspended their freedoms and outsourced moral decisions to the state. Without so much as a whisper of opposition.'

'The long term damage to our socio economic health is at this point immeasurable. There's no question but that we're heading into a monumental abyss.'

'It's an adults' game of 'Blind Mans Buff'. Politicians are wedded to their narrative come hell or high water.'

'Covidiocy... should go in the dictionary. Sucking on the teat... no sucking here unless it's bloody oxygen to keep the business alive.'

'It's staggering and heartbreaking to see so many young people, who have worked so hard, feel totally abandoned at this critical time.'

'This 'government' is absolutely revolting beyond words, how do they sleep at night?'

'I've given up on the British press, so I am very grateful for your regular sane summaries of what's going on there.'

'We have to man up a lot, and quite soon, or there will not be much economy left.'

# Also from Ed Wood

**From Acorns**
Read Ed Wood's memoir 'From Acorns', a riveting account of how the worlds of business, politics and family have changed over half a century—and how we should change to keep up with them.

Second Edition.
Publication date: 27<sup>th</sup> June 2021

'A wonderfully uplifting and tender book. Wood's love for that extraordinary, wide-ranging, cast of characters that make up the narrative of his professional, social and family life is unmistakable and also humbling. Reading this book at a time when love, above all things, matters more than ever and when one's mind is concentrated on the very essentials, has been an inspiring experience'.

— Juliet Nicolson, author of The Perfect Summer, The Great Silence, Abdication, Memory & Desire, A House full of Daughters and Frostquake

What people have said about *From Acorns*

'Reading this book was like taking a walk with an old friend, ending up in the pub, and putting the world to rights over a pint.'

'Eloquent, brutally honest, thought-provoking and inspirational. Read it.'

'It is a rare treat to read a memoir like 'From Acorns'—a life full of drama, laughter and occasional mischief, told in Ed's inimitable irreverent voice.'

'Adventure, love, family, friends, business and infectious humour shine through each crafted page. This is meaty, close to the bone, with red-blooded views and blue-blooded people.'

'Ed Wood has lived an amazing life, from a family of famous politicians to finding his own place in the world. His early struggles, his youthful adventures, his business ups and downs and personal trials, bought me both to laughter and tears.'

'A fascinating journey through a world that seems to have been lost forever. Ed's life is a living history of the world as it changes. He has an infectious optimism even when life sometimes throws up its worst.'

# About Ed Wood

Ed wrote *Lift Off!*—his business autobiography—to help Entrepreneurs to navigate the many obstacles of business life, having fallen into countless pooh traps, and been up the ladders—and down the snakes—over a near 50 year business career. Wood qualified as a Chartered

Accountant in the early 1980s, and, later, as a Commercial Helicopter Pilot (thus the name of this book: *Lift Off!*). He has helped many small to medium sized businesses, hands on, over that time. *Lift Off!* is available from 2nd May, 2020.

Wood also wrote a daily diary during the horrors of Coronavirus. Every day, he became increasingly aghast at the UK government's staggering mishandling of Covid, its manufacturing of fear, its curtailment of the people's freedoms and its ruination of the economy. So, *Plague of Madness* was born, also to be published in May, 2020.

Ed had already written a personal autobiography in 2018. He decided to talk about everything that had ever happened to him, good or bad, sad or funny, and, to his amazement, found that the book was very well received when he published it, as *From Acorns*, early in 2018. A second edition will come out in June 2020, because he has had over two years to remember other bits of his life which he forgot to write about earlier.

When he is not writing, Ed runs Runway Advisors (www.runwayadvisors.co.uk), which he founded in 2019—a collective of 30 specialists, each an expert in their own profession. Runway Advisors exists to help entrepreneurs to make more money and have more fun doing it.

He, and his wife Katha, moved from Gloucestershire to Andalucia at the end 2020, with their four beloved terriers and Katha's mixed herd of horses and ponies. A new journey has begun.

Lightning Source UK Ltd.
Milton Keynes UK
UKHW040640180521
383923UK00001B/176